The Great Debate

By

Rayola Kelley

(Exposing Man's Great Debacle)

Hidden Manna Publications

The Great Debate

(Exposing Man's Great Debacle)

Copyright © 2020 by Rayola Kelley

ISBN: 978-0-9864066-9-0

Cover Design: Pam Wester

Printed in the USA

Except where otherwise indicated, all Scripture quotations in this book are taken from the King James Version of the Bible.

Hidden Manna Publications
PO Box 3572
Oldtown, ID 83822

Facebook:
https://www.facebook.com/HiddenMannaPublications/

Dedication

I want to **dedicate** this book to a special group of men who have challenged and inspired me at the different stages of my life in different ways.

To my brother **David Kelley:** We have been through many adventures together in our youth, became friends in our teenage years, found our different paths as adults, and in spite of the changes, you have always tried to be the best brother a girl could ask for. Thank you for the impossible task of always trying to be there for me at the right time and in the right way.

Mike Kropp: You have been such a wonderful pillar who has a gentle spirit, a big heart, and a wonderful way of upholding those around you while sharing your deep love for God and your strong Scriptural convictions. I so appreciate your faithful friendship and support through the years and the priceless nuggets you have always joyfully set before me to enrich my life.

Fred O'Brien: You started out as a great boss who taught me bookkeeping and you graduated to becoming an indelible example of what it means to always seek to see a person's potential, encourage them to reach their heights, and patiently lend a hand to help them realize it. You are the one who told me I needed to be in full-time ministry because you could see the desire of my heart. Now I call you friend and thank the Lord for putting you in my path at the right time of my life, as well as forever grateful to you for challenging me to look in the right direction.

James Stewart: I have watched your struggle to reach great heights in God. Your desire to be a godly man in your conduct and a man of

God's Word in action reveals much about your heart towards your Creator. You have often struggled to climb high mountains, scale rock cliffs, reach tall pinnacles, and cross over tough canyons on a tight rope, and in spite of how many times you have been knocked back, you have never given up, surrendered, and turned back. Your determination to be a man of God serves as an example of what it will take to come forth with a refined faith and a strong testimony.

Acknowledgement

I want to thank Wanda
Hiebert for proof reading this book,
along with my co-laborer,
Jeannette Haley for her commitment
to see me through each book
including this one.

Contents

Introduction

This book is about the great debate--the deliberation that has been taking place, to some extent, ever since the Garden of Eden, and has escalated more so as man toils in the spiritual wilderness of this world. In man's mind if he works hard, lives decently, treats his neighbor with consideration, keeps his word, and tries to do good, life should treat him pretty well. After all, he has earned it.

However, man finds that at the heart of life is a tragedy that he can't reconcile in his mind. This tragedy shakes all that he thinks he understands about God and life as it flies in the face of everything that seems logical and fair to him. And, what is this great tragedy? It is "that bad things can happen to good people."

The truth is because mankind lives under a curse brought on all by the actions of our first parents in Genesis 3, the tragedy of sorrow, great toil, loss, and despair plagues every man in one way or the other as he faces circumstances and happenings that are beyond his control; and yet, if he believes in the God of heaven, he understands that all events are under His control. This is where the debate can hit—when reality collides with our philosophy that is often based on our sense of right and wrong. Highs of passionate sentiments rise to great peaks in those who have sought to understand the matter, leading them to conclusions they perceive should be obvious to any thinking individual. Peaks of arrogance will always cause the person who is experiencing a crisis to descend into utter despair because nothing makes sense as they try to answer that simple question, "How can a just God allow bad things to happen to good people?"

In man's attempt to delve into this matter, he often hits greater confusion that finds its springboard in fear of the unexplainable, the unrecognizable, and the unknown. Either he must choose to trust in the goodness of God in the midst of what seems to be thick darkness in which the loving, committed Creator appears to be silent and indifferent, or curse Him and walk away from Him in great anger and despair.

The beauty about God is that He takes this issue head on in one book, the book of Job. However, it seems that the message, explanation, or hope of Job has become lost in some theological circles causing the great debate in the book of Job to become "The Great Debacle" when presented as a teaching. In some cases, Bible teachers stay away from the book altogether, or they fall back on the old "stale narratives" developed by past theologians that prove weak and leave one frustrated, spiritually anemic, or close to being insulted. Sadly, some of the accepted and popular theological interpretations of the book of Job that I have been exposed to lack real perspective, are clearly void of any inspiration, and fail to properly bring people back to the real issue of the matter.

It is important to point out that Job is not only considered to be the oldest book in the Bible, but it is also the first book in the five poetic books that are located in the middle of the 66 books of what is also known as the Canon. It is poetic because it deals with the philosophical points of life that arouse great debates among those who are trying to answer a few mysterious questions surrounding life. At such times, even the most honest presentations, while trying to climb the logical steps of deductive reasoning, can hit the lows of despair. At other times it can appear as if the summit of a pinnacle has been reached, only to find oneself teetering at the top before plunging into a freefall where there is no assurance of the landing, or else quickly sliding down into greater darkness of uncertainty

In spite of the up and down swings of the debate that often seem redundant to many, Job often lands on the runway of faith to continue to stand on the character of God in light of His promises. It is for this reason, Job is a great book of promise as it answers some very fundamental questions, but to recognize the answers, the reader must avoid getting caught up with the logical part of the debate, and constantly come back to the crux of the matter that was clearly set up within the first two chapters of Job and clearly summarized in the last chapter of Job. In fact, the book of Job has reminded me that if I do not start from the premise laid out in the first two chapters, and make sure my conclusions line up to the final deduction as presented by the Lord Himself, then I have missed the real message and lessons of Job.

The question is, are you ready to step into the whirlwind of the debate in order to land securely on the truth in order to glean the answers that will put to rest "the Great Debate?"

The Lord may not have planned that this
(circumstance) overtake me, but He has most
certainly permitted it. Therefore though
it were an attack of an enemy, by the
time it reaches me, it has the Lord's permission
and therefore all is well. He will make
it work together with all life's
experiences for good.
(Unknown)

1

The Matter of Debate

Answers to all my questions: there have been
none. If I had answers...then I guess there
would be no use for faith and hope! I'm
hoping in the unseen. Faith is being
sure of what we hope for and certain
of what we do not see.
(Mary Beth Chapman)

It may seem a bit unusual to start with the subject of "debate". After all, the book of Job is one big debate, but I believe it is of the utmost importance to start from this premise in order to properly discern how God views debate.

This may seem a bit unusual, but it will set up an important foundation as we look at the debate that went on between Job and his companions. By beginning with the premise of how God views debate, we will have a better means of discerning whether such method is profitable to the soul.

In the world, debate is an art, a type of craft that is to be fine-tuned in order to successfully debate in the different arenas of the world. Consider the debate teams in schools and colleges and the pride that is put forth to win the debate. Other arenas where great debates can become, for what the world considers to be the best platform for the great orators of the age to shine, are in the halls of Congress and in the courtrooms.

Another arena for debate is religion. In the past, I have debated where the Word of God was concerned. I must say I took much pride in my presentations. Oh, how wise I appeared in my own eyes and in my mind, I could only imagine how smart I must have sounded to everyone else. Admittedly, I was too impressed with myself to realize it was a matter of conceit and had nothing to do with intelligence or wisdom.[1]

As I watched the debates that often take place in the different arenas of the world, I had to note a couple of hard-hitting facts. First of all, the debate is much more about the art and not about the substance. Case in point, debate teams are sometimes given the subject that they are to defend. It does not matter if they agree or not because it is about the art of debating.

The second fact I had to recognize about debate is that it is all about controlling the narrative, not coming to a real consensus as to if something is valid or not. The art of debate is whether you can outtalk the opponent in order to push him or her in a corner of silence so you can appear as if you have come out on top in the argument. Once again, it is not about substance but about the craft, the art of debate.

The third thing I had to recognize about debate that proved to be the most disturbing aspect of it to me, is that the real goal behind debate has nothing to do with coming to truth. Debate couldn't care less about truth. It is not seeking it, nor is it interested in it. In many cases, the facts of truth get in the way of debate that operates in the realm of fantasy as it often paints a picture of fanciful notions and wishful thinking to impress or persuade the listener who might not be established in his or her opinion about the subject. Debate rarely deals in reality as it ignores facts and skips over any attempts to reason a matter out on an equal playing field of honest discussion. It often flies high on emotional

---

[1] Romans 12:16

sentiment, and has no intention of listening to the opponents unless it is for the sole purpose of debasing or intimidating them. When it appears that the debaters are running out of arguments and time, in utter desperation they resort to the lowest tactics that are often childish, rude, ludicrous, accusing, insulting, and downright insane.

As you watch debaters swing from branches of fanciful notions to the zealous branch of passion, and watch rage take hold of the highest branch of arrogance, while looking down with utter disdain on those whom they now consider to be too inept and stupid to see that they are right, I believe there is an ever so faint reality check that they are not winning on the basis of ideology. Although passionate about the subject, they still have failed to win converts. Such an indication can ramp up their emotional fervor even more so because they still must have the last word to come out the victor, causing them to resort to their last final, foul attempt to come out on top. Socrates summarized this last attempt in this statement, "When the debate is lost, slander becomes the tool of the losers."

The question is, can you find the concept of debate in Scripture? The word "debate" is used only five times in the King James Version. Needless to say, the word is not used in a positive light. To avoid a matter from becoming gossip in Proverbs 25:9, one is to go to his neighbor and debate or present his or her situation to him before a matter gets out of hand. In Isaiah 27:8, debate is used in the case of Israel wanting to complain, contend, rebuke, plead, or strive with the Lord concerning the judgment coming upon the nation due to sin. In Isaiah 58:1-4, the people of Israel had an outward show of piousness and repentance through prayer and fasting to bolster their debate with God, while still holding to wicked ways and practices. In Romans 1:29, the word debate, which is associated with strife and contention, was named among the sins that were linked with those who possessed a reprobate mind towards the things of God. The Apostle Paul lumped this practice with the foul ways of the flesh in 2 Corinthians 12:20-21,

> For I fear, lest, when I come, I shall not find you such as I would, and *that* I shall be found unto you such as ye would not: lest *there be* debates, envyings, wraths, strifes, backbitings, whisperings, swellings, tumults: *And* lest, when I come again, my God will humble me among you, and *that* I shall bewail many which have sinned already, and have not repented of the uncleanness and fornication and lasciviousness which they have committed.

This brings us to an important conclusion: debate is a fleshly exercise. It proves to be unprofitable because without truth it can't edify, without care for the soul it can't encourage, without the right spirit it has no real authority or power, and without eternal significance it proves to be a useless exercise. It is for this reason the Apostle Paul gave this instruction in Philippians 2:3, "Let nothing *be done* through strife or vainglory; but in lowliness of mind let each esteem other better than themselves."

The exercise of debate clearly has no place in the kingdom of God. In Ephesians 6:10-17, we are told to stand, withstand, and continue to stand in our armor, which includes the belt of truth. When you are standing, there is no debate taking place. You are standing in order to face the enemy, withstanding in order to not be moved from what is rightfully your authority and inheritance, as well as continue to stand because you will not allow yourself to be robbed of what is true, and will ultimately prove to be so in the end. Finally, we are told after sanctifying the Lord in our hearts, we are to be ready to give an answer of the hope in us with meekness and fear in 1 Peter 3:15.

When you look up the word, "answer" in the Strong's Concordance, it points to giving an account, which is a legal plea or a type of defense.[2]   In other words, you present your case based on facts that you know to be true. In such a presentation, there is no debate because it requires a determination or judgment call based on what was presented and what is known to be true.

Debate is not only fleshly, but it can be traced back to the great tempter. The Bible gives us a clear presentation of how Satan and his system works. John 8:44 tells us that Satan is the father of lies and a murderer from the beginning. In 2 Corinthians 4:2, we are told, "But have renounced the hidden things of dishonesty, not walking in craftiness, nor handling the word of God deceitfully; but by manifestation of the truth commending ourselves to every man's conscience in the sight of God."

The word, "craftiness" in this text points to shrewdness that is misleading because it entails trickery and subtilty.[3] There is treachery behind such craftiness that is intended to seduce in a contrived attempt to influence and determine one's worldview. It is to condition one in order to indoctrinate one into a different reality that is quite contrary to one's personal conscience, reason, and moral beliefs. It is for this reason, Christians are given this instruction in Ephesians 4:14, "That we *henceforth* be no more children, tossed to and fro, and carried about with every wind of doctrine, by the sleight of men, *and* cunning craftiness, whereby they lie in wait to deceive." Notice how the enemy is lying in wait for the right opportunity to deceive by carefully laying the right trap that we are innocently prone to fall into. It is for this reason the Apostle Paul instructed the Corinthians in this way, "Lest Satan should get an advantage of us: for we are not ignorant of his devices" (2 Corinthians 2:11).

The enemy of our soul is after our minds. He knows that, like Eve in the Garden of Eden in Genesis 3:1-6, once he can magnify

---

[2] Strong's Exhaustive Concordance of the Bible, #626 & 627
[3] Ibid, #3834

something in our minds as being important to our happiness, necessary to live by, and desirable to possess, he can seduce us into another reality, while humanizing God in some way in order to replace Him with an idolatrous image that he hides behind.

Satan is the god of this age and as I considered how Satan works according to his craft of deception, I began to realize that "debate" belongs to his world. It is clearly in line with his art of deceiving. Debate is one of his devices he effectively uses in this world. His goal and ability to come out on top of truth by slowly murdering it with small cuts of lies, while wearing down the resolve of his opponents in such a way that they will be afraid to stand on truth. As his opponents are being worn down, they can easily become too intimidated to stand for it, as well as ashamed of it, or uncertain about whether it is worth standing and dying for in the arenas of the world. The devil must be clever in his seduction and subtle in his conditioning, while giving a noble appearance that his deceitful presentation is for the "greater good" of everyone. He desires to blind us to the Gospel so we remain in darkness, under condemnation and doomed in our ways.[4] Satan's goal is to knock out the light of truth by creating a false narrative in order to capture the mind with fantasy while enslaving the heart with unrealistic notions that will leave one ultimately devastated, angry, and an utter skeptic towards all matters of God, life, and morality.

As we consider this "Great Debate," in the book of Job, we must ask who started it, what was the spirit behind those who propagated it, and what were the fruits of it?

---

[4] 2 Corinthians 4:3,4; 10:3-5; 11:1-14; 1 Timothy 4:1,2

2

The Arenas

*Trials are used to purify you; it is the fiery
furnace of affliction that God uses to get
you in the place where He can use you. The
person who has no trials and no difficulties
is the person whom God does not dare allow
Satan to touch because the person could
not stand temptation.
(Smith Wigglesworth)*

Since we have considered the issue of debate, we must consider the arenas where this debate took place in the book of Job. This is vital if we are to keep centered to the real issues and follow the line of truth that will bring us to a proper conclusion.

There were three arenas in which this great debate took place. The first arena started in a type of judgment hall where an incredible throne stood. I say this because the one who starts this debate does so with an accusation or a supposition before the great judge of the universe. This courtroom scene is set up in Job 1:6, "Now there was a day when the sons of God came to present themselves before the LORD, and Satan came also among them."

We begin with the presentation of the Judge and the accuser. In every debate there must be two sides to develop a case. It is important for the reader to realize the debate that is about to ensue did not start on earth, but in heaven. Since it began in the unseen realm, this debate can't be reasoned out on an intellectual level because there will be some important facts that will be missing from it that could easily enough change the narrative.

In a way the man, Job who stood accused during the debate, sensed that there were events consuming his life that possessed an element that remained hidden, but were never considered. Through the whole debate this one unseen element that would have changed and silenced the great debate was never outrightly alluded to, revealing that the debate would ultimately be derailed; therefore, doomed.

The one fact that I wrestle with every time the book of Job is discussed is, even though the readers are presented with this fact, they seem to end up on the same old train that is bound to be derailed by truth. Instead of standing on the real crux of the matter, many still take the side of Job's companions and come out with the same suppositions as they came to in their conclusions. However, what did the Lord make clear about Job's conclusions when he spoke to Job's friend Eliphaz and his two companions in Job 42:7c? "My wrath is kindled against thee, and against thy two friends: for ye have not spoken of me *the thing that is* right, as my servant Job *hath*."

As a reminder, this is God's conclusion to the matter. What do we know? First, the Lord is talking to the first three companions who knew Job and had presented their cases. He is very clear that they were wrong and Job was right in his presentation. Now there was a fourth companion by the name of Elihu that did not personally know Job and it becomes clear that he was either persuaded to agree with Job's companions in the debate, or he had come to like conclusions on his own. One can only reason that even though this man is not mentioned with the other three companions in the Lord's rebuke, that if he took the side of Job's companions that he also was wrong because Job was right. I believe that Elihu received a personal rebuke, but we will deal with that possibility later on in the book.

This brings us to the second courtroom, that of the world. The world can be considered a courtroom where God is on trial, or a classroom where man is being tested. As a courtroom, we already know for the most part the judgments leveled at God along with His truth and righteousness will be perverted to fit the world's narrative. Jesus said in John 7:7, "The world cannot hate you; but me it hateth, because I testify of it, that the works thereof are evil." He later made this statement on the night He was betrayed in John 17:14, "I have given them thy word; and the world hath hated them, because they are not of the world, even as I am not of the world."

The world is always presenting a case against God and His Word. It has done everything to strip God of His sovereignty in the minds of those who dare to believe in Him, while mocking the authority of His servants, downplaying the power of His Word and redefining His perfect ways. The truth is, the world is always trying to wipe out the witness of God. It will despise His truth, rage against His righteousness, and try to destroy any credible witnesses.

The third arena where all debates take place is in man's mind. Man perceives he must understand before he believes, but the truth is he must choose to believe God's Word before the Holy Spirit can bring him to any understanding.[1] Man uses logic to reinforce what he knows, while God desires to reason with man about those things which he is blind towards to bring revelation to him.[2]

Man's logic is limited to what he can see and understand, and it is for this reason, he is ever adjusting all matters to fit within his logic. On the other hand, God's reasoning allows man to step outside of personal boxes so he can ultimately see outside of the box. I recently read a statement that summarizes this truth, "Faith

---

[1] 1 Corinthians 2:10-14
[2] Isaiah 1:18

accepts God's Word as it is, waits for the event, sure that it will clear up all difficulties."

Man's limited understanding towards the unseen will bring him into a place of complete darkness about what is, and it is only by clinging to what he knows about God's character that he will be able to walk through the darkness. When he finally comes to the light that causes all darkness to lift, that is when he will be allowed to see his faith towards God was not in vain.

In the courtroom of heaven, Satan uses accusations, while in the courtroom of the world, such things as tribulation and circumstances puts man on the search to understand the "whys" behind such events, only to find himself being ushered into the dark night of the soul. It is such conclusions that can become strongholds in the mind.[3] The mind is where man turns to logic to explain the unexplainable and that which appears to be unjust. This causes both to become a platform where doubt becomes the persecutor, speculation takes the stand, supposition is presented, logic serves as the jury, and personal conclusions the judgment.

Any judgments made during such a debate take place in the mind, and it is from this premise that an individual can't even imagine how he could be wrong about his conclusion. After all it makes perfect sense to him. However, the Bible warns that what we often think is light is darkness, while arrogance allows us to "supposedly" confirm it by thinking highly of ourselves. In fact, when we think we are standing, we are in reality about to fall flat on our face.[4] Another way of putting it, we end up with mud on our face, eating crow.

This brings us to the question: can we trust the debates taking place in the last two courtrooms? Even in the first one, the challenge is based on accusation from the enemy of God and our

---

[3] 2 Corinthians 10:3-5
[4] Matthew 6:22,23; Romans 12:3; 1 Corinthians 10:12

souls. The answer is no, we cannot, which means we must begin with what happened in the courtroom of heaven.

This brings us to the case. We need to understand what the real crux of the case is before we can discern the points of the debate. It is important to point out that the case was really leveled at God, and it resulted in one man's soul becoming the battleground between God and Satan.

The Case

The case began with a challenge from Satan. It started with God pointing out a man to His enemy. Now I want you to consider this fact for a moment. For God to point out one man would no doubt put a target on this man's back where Satan was concerned.

The question is why did God point this man out to the enemy? Keep in mind, the main reason Satan stands before God is to bring accusation against believers, and his goal in this case was to convince God that if all was taken away from one of His devoted followers, and if the only thing left was a choice between clinging to God by faith or cursing and flinging such faith aside to become a reprobate, that such an individual would inevitably choose to become a reprobate.[5]

I realize the presentation of this challenge may be a bit simple, but that is what it came down to. Consider the scene in heaven. Satan presented himself before the throne of God with the other angels. The Lord asked Satan where had he come from. He admitted that he was going to and fro in the earth, and from walking up and down in it. The question is, why?[6]

Remember, Satan is the accuser of the people of God. It was clear he was roaming the earth to find someone whom he could

---

[5] 2 Corinthians 13:5
[6] Job 1:7

accuse and maybe even devour.[7] It was after Satan's answer that the Lord made this statement in Job 1:8, "Hast thou considered my servant Job?"

It is easy for Satan to build a case against any man because for the most part, Satan is correct. Allow him to touch aspects of any man's life, and that man will, in good time, turn and curse his Creator for his grave plight. Even though God did not bring such wickedness on man, the suffering soul will question God's upright intention, godly character, and perfect ways. He will rage against Him for the fruits of wickedness, the death and destruction it leaves behind, and the utter despair it leaves mankind in. I know this is true because I have heard such rages.

The important point here is that Job is not just any man. The Lord referred to him as His servant. Clearly, God knew Job and Job knew God. When a person is considered a servant, his life is not his own to do as he will. A servant belongs to his or her lord. In this case, Job knew his life was not his own, and that he was at the beck and call of his Lord.

As we will see, God was not pointing Job out because there was something wrong in his character; rather, He was pointing him out to Satan because Job had impeccable character because of his faith towards Him. Satan is jealous of God and strives to exalt himself above his Creator. His goal is to prove to God that unless He placates man, He will discover that man will turn on Him just as he did in Ezekiel 28:14-19. This is important to understand that what Satan was implying to God is that unless man benefits from his Creator, he will see no need to love, worship, or serve Him. Man must be bribed at the point of his self-serving ways, coddled to ensure his fragile feelings are not toppled, and his pride pacified before he will have anything good to say about God, and give Him any real consideration. At this point, it would be well for us to

---

[7] 1 Peter 5:8

remember that when everything goes right for man, he usually forgets God, and perceives he is self-sufficient, infallible, worthy, and elite, which, in his mind, makes him immune from any real tragedies and consequences of life.

This idea that God must keep man happy for him to serve Him was brought out when Satan asked a simple question, "Doth Job fear God for nought? Hast not thou made an hedge about him, and about his house, and about all that he hath on every side? thou hast blessed the work of his hands, and his substance is increased in the land."[8] Think about the accusation that is being leveled at God at this point. Satan was saying no man would think Him worthy of worship and service without the benefits.

However, God is worthy of worship and service regardless of whether man perceives he is benefitting in his relationship with Him. We can see such worship in every arena. Consider the example and tone happening around the throne in Revelation 4:9-11,

> And when those beasts give glory and honour and thanks to him that sat on the throne, who liveth for ever and ever, The four and twenty elders fall down before him that sat on the throne, and worship him that liveth for ever and ever, and cast their crowns before the throne, saying, Thou art worthy, O Lord, to receive glory and honour and power: for thou hast created all things, and for thy pleasure they are and were created.

Paul and Silas worshipped God within prison walls, David worshipped God in his many psalms when he was running from Saul, and Daniel paid homage to God, knowing full well it could cost him his life.[9]

---

[8] Job 1:9b-10
[9] Daniel 6:5-11; Acts 16:25-31

There are many stories of such worship taking place in the most challenging arenas of the world. Real worship is not about whether man thinks God is worthy of such consideration; rather, it is about properly honoring the one true God who is worthy of all worship, regardless of Satan's attempts to stop it and man's rejection of God in his life. We actually see the culmination of this worship being executed by all in Philippians 2:9-11,

> Wherefore God also hath highly exalted him, and given him a name which is above every name: That at the name of Jesus every knee should bow, of *things* in heaven, and *things* in earth, and *things* under the earth; And *that* every tongue should confess that Jesus Christ *is* Lord, to the glory of God the Father.

The key is that the natural response of the spiritual man towards God, regardless of the circumstances, will be worship. Job was no exception. We are told in Job 1:20-21 after losing much,

> Then Job arose, and rent his mantle, and shaved his head, and fell down upon the ground, and worshipped, And said, Naked came I out of my mother's womb, and naked shall I return thither: the LORD gave, and the LORD hath taken away; blessed be the name of the LORD.

Satan is forever trying to undermine the character and authority of God by putting doubt on His intentions and character. The devil tries to make God out to be some mean, cruel, unfair tyrant. The problem is man weighs a matter based on what he thinks is fair and not in light of the fact that all of God's judgments are righteous and will prove to be so in the end.

I understand man's sense of justice bringing him to wrong conclusions about the unseen matters of heaven. I remember as a young Christian, trying to logic out in my mind that if I was serving God, I would be immune from challenges of life. However, there was a time when the challenges were great and overwhelming to me. The path I was on was hard and the way was made difficult by many devastating obstacles. This caused a type of self-pity to come over me, and in nearly a whining tone I asked God how He could allow this to happen. You know what happened next? He answered me with a Scripture found in Matthew 5:45, "That ye may be the children of your Father which is in heaven: for he maketh his sun to rise on the evil and on the good, and sendeth rain on the just and on the unjust."

As I read the Bible, I discovered a pattern. Just before God's people entered into His blessings and promises, they encountered great hardness, testing, or affliction. It is a pattern that constantly plays out. Consider the Israelites just before they entered the Promised land, they were murmuring that the way was hard. There was Peter who was told the night Jesus was betrayed that Satan would be sifting him, but He had prayed for him and when he was converted, he was to go to the others and comfort them. There was Paul and his great encounter on the road to Damascus where he lost his eyesight and was told of the things he would suffer for the sake of Christ. The greatest example we have is Jesus. He was lifted up by a cross, and put into a grave and three day later He arose in resurrection power.[10]

This brings us to the test. As I have told you, the world is a courtroom in which God is being constantly accused by man, but for man it is a classroom where he will be tested time and again. The question is what is on the line for a man such as Job? Jude 3 answers that question, "Beloved, when I gave all diligence to write unto you of the common salvation, it was needful for me to write unto you, and exhort *you* that ye should earnestly **contend for the faith** which was once delivered unto the saints." (Emphasis added.)

---

[10] Numbers 21:4-9; Luke 22:31,32; Acts 9:3-16

Job's faith was Satan's target. He knew if he could get Job to give up his faith towards God, that his accusations leveled against man would be confirmed. I often wondered if Satan thinks that every time a person of God is toppled in his life, witness, or faith that it justifies his own deviant actions to reject God's authority as a means to exalt himself as God.

We know according to 1 Peter 1:5-9 that our faith must go through a refinement process to be brought forth as pure gold. Faith **towards** God is what allows us to stand in the tests, faith **in** God's character is what allows us to patiently withstand when we are under attack, and our faith **established** in God is what allows us to continue to stand in expectation of promises being brought forth in our lives.

What we must keep in mind is that faith begins where our understanding ceases. It is a choice and when it is first challenged, it can waver easily enough until the person steps back and chooses to step over the emotional shock of the challenging mountain before him or her. Faith will question until the person is assured that the problem does not rest with him or her. It will wrestle before God until it can come to a place of confidence that it is a test and not a matter of chastisement. In times of weakness the saint can fall into despair, but he or she will choose to look beyond personal inabilities and begin to trust in the greatness of God's character and not the circumstances. In darkness, the believer will choose to cling to God's faithfulness and not how he or she feels. The patient saint knows that he or she must climb over the doubts of uncertainties in order to catch the wind of the Spirit that will take them above the circumstances and bring them safely to the place of rest in the Lord.

This is another reason I love the book of Job, because it does just that. Job digs deep into the "whys" of the matter, wrestles with what looks like the senselessness of the situation, and climbs above what appears to be the obvious to the rational man to always hold onto unseen truths of God, while patiently enduring a mountain of accusations in order to land on the runway of faith.

The book of Job shows me the integrity and enduring qualities of real faith. Faith is not something that simply shows up as some great deliverer; rather, faith is measured out each time a person simply chooses to believe in what God's has said to be true, trusts God's faithful character in the times of great darkness, and comes to a place of assurance that God remains immutable in all things.[11]

Once again, I want to encourage the reader not to get caught up with the logical aspects of this debate, but to consider Job's faith as he wrestles with his own humanness in a time of great adversity that was brought on by the unseen realm of Satan. This test was not to bring out some flaw in Job's character, but to put the spotlight on his faith. This test not only brought out the character of Job's faith as a means to confirm what God already knew, but it served as a testimony to Satan, that once the fire of adversity is put to unfeigned faith it is not consumed; rather, it is refined to such a state that it will ultimately reflect the very glory of God.

---

[11] Malachi 3:6; Romans 10:17; 12:3; Titus 1:2; Hebrews 11:6; 13:8

3

Perspective

God had a very specific purpose in
allowing Job to suffer as He did. His
purpose was that Job would be a model
for all generations after him of how
God's ways are beyond comprehension,
of how the righteous suffer, and of
God's designs to bring them through
to victory.
(Bob Sorge)

Perspective is everything. It is the premise from which one begins to weigh or analyze the facts and challenges in light of calculations that are based on various factors. These factors can include family traditions, teachings, cultural and religious influences, and experiences.

Most people utilize logic up front to come to some conclusion. The problem with intellectual logic is that it rationalizes a matter based on what appears to be obvious to the physical eye. Logic for the most part is based on what is tangible and does not have the liberty to move outside of the established boundaries, which will always bring conclusions back to the original premise of understanding.[1] In fact, the main purpose of logic is to confirm what one suspects to be so, regardless of facts. Keep in mind, logic will decide that known facts have changed and the reason

---

[1] 1 Corinthians 1:21-28

the rational individual knows that it is true is because the facts do not fit into what he or she sees or perceives as being true at that time. Therefore, the facts must be discarded and the logical conclusion upheld.

The other aspect of logic is that it sees spiritual insight as being insane. It can't relate to it or even give it a slight consideration because it can't imagine trusting in the unseen when the material world makes sense to all of the human senses. We see this rationalism operating in a man name Festus in Acts 26:24. The Apostle Paul was trying to contend with Agrippa and Festus by giving his testimony about the risen Christ and this was the rationalized response of Festus, "Paul, thou art beside thyself; much learning doth make thee mad."

Another premise people use are feelings. It is all about how something makes them feel. Once again, feelings couldn't care less about the facts or truth of a matter. Feelings find their inspiration in sentiment, and for this reason it tests something based on how it affects the person. Individuals who are depending on feelings to determine their reality are looking to be pampered and placated but never challenged. They clearly want to feel good about every decision they make and every deed they do. Without feelings these people have no real inspiration and motivation to stand or pursue a matter, and when feelings are challenged in a negative way, these fickle individuals will quickly take offense and cry, "foul." Since these people work off the temperamental gauge of emotions, they can go immediately from being cold to the hot passion of indignation.

Jesus clearly encountered this temperamental sentiment from those who followed Him. In John 6, Jesus stated a hard truth, causing some of His followers to become uneasy, unsure, and insulted. Jesus' sayings clearly inserted themselves into any fanciful notions His fickle followers had about being part of His group. John 6:66 tells us what happened, "From that *time* many of his disciples went back, and walked no more with him." Those who operate from the emotional, fickle sentiment, never make for good disciples. They rarely finish the course because much of the Christian walk does not feel pleasant, nor will it feed fragile egos. The reality is that truth will offend individuals who may possess any self-serving agendas or sentimental notions about following Jesus, causing a cutting away that will find them flinging aside any commitment to continue down the same path.

The next avenue man uses is reasoning. Logic is a form of reasoning, but it is one sided. In logic man reasons a matter out in his personal courtroom of understanding. True reasoning is when one reasons with another to come to a viable conclusion about what is really going on. The only time that reasoning with another is used in relationship to logic is when the "rational" person is trying to get the "blinded" individual, due to ignorance or stupidity, to see what is clearly rational. At such times it is not about coming to a real understanding as to what is going on; rather, it is about getting the "blind" person to see it your way.

Isaiah 1:18 declares that God desires to reason with us over the matter of sin, which brings us to the difference between intellectual logic and reasoning. Unlike intellectual logic, reason deals in reality. It starts from the premise of truth in order to properly examine the facts of a situation. The purpose of such reasoning is to bring a person to a place of, not only acknowledging the matter at hand, but to deal with it.

You can't deal with a problem unless it is brought to the light and honestly faced. Those who are part of the problem must own their part before any real change will occur. The Apostle Paul made clear that all works of darkness must be brought to the light and reproved.[2]

---

[2] Ephesians 5:10-13

Man must make sure his conclusion rings true no matter what. In the case of debate, if one presentation does not work, he will bring it from another angle. It is natural for man to focus on many different things from diverse angles in order to answer the questions that make no sense to his logic. The problem is that man's conclusions can be quite different from each other and the reason for this is because he is looking either from the top down, from the bottom up or from a side angle.

The truth is if you are looking down, you have to consider from what height. There is a saying, "A person can't see the forest for the trees." Mankind rarely will ever get beyond the tree line to see the forest. He might be looking down from a knoll or from some other elevated spot, but his perspective remains limited to what he can see. In reality, he is still looking at the same trees along the same tree line.

This was true for three of Job's companion. These three men personally knew Job as a friend, but now they had found themselves in an elevated spot, but it was not from some grand height. Keep in mind these men sat silently with Job for seven days before the verbal debate started.[3] Can you imagine the great debate that took place in their minds? The facts of what they knew about the character of Job was not lining up to the evil circumstances that had engulfed him.

It was clear to them that none of it made sense unless the facts had changed. Since the immutable God would not bring such evil devastation on a person without good reason, then there was something in Job that brought this on him, and as his friends, they had the responsibility to get him to see it so God "could withdraw His heavy hand" from their friend.

Sadly, their elevation was based on the same ground of knowledge, but now they stood above the matter because of the

---

[3] Job 2:11-13

great depth that Job found himself falling into because of his personal plight. Job's companions were simply evaluating a matter from the same position as before without realizing it. Regardless of what angle a person approaches the matter, he or she will see the same tree line and come up with the same conclusions.

The safest position, but the most challenging place of the three perspectives, is to be on the bottom looking up. Granted, one might only see the gravity of the situation and wrestle with the "whys" of it while pushing through its darkness, but the person is more apt to come out with a realistic conclusion. After all, the first group thinks they know what is going on because they see the terrain of circumstances, as in the case of Job's companions, but for the one on the bottom, this particular individual sees nothing but the darkness and the only thing that can part such darkness is the light of what is real and true.

Finally, we have the third angle, the side angle. This angle points to those who are merely observers. They sit on the sideline and observe the debate. For the most part they are quiet because they might be confused about the situation, or too fearful to speak their mind, or they think themselves too clever or wise to speak to a matter and have no intention of allowing their high opinion of themselves to be challenged or changed. There are also those who may have come along just for show or out of curiosity, but underneath they really do not care about the real matter and will eventually become bored with it.

However, those who take an interest in it do so to somehow judge it. They may convince themselves that they are there to learn from a matter, but in reality, they are there to not only judge a matter but weigh in on it. The problem with observers of this kind is that they eventually become referees that will yell "foul," as they judge the matter from the sidelines. After all, they have watched the whole situation unravel before them and have seen where the losing "team" went wrong.

This was true for Elihu. He did not know Job on a personal level. However, he had quietly listened to the debate and became angry at Job's other three companions because they did not convince Job of what had become apparent to him. Consider what Job 32:5 tells us, "When Elihu saw that *there was* no answer in the mouth of *these* three men, then his wrath was kindled."

Needless to say, when a person such as Elihu is given center stage, he will get into the mix like any observer to set the record straight. In fact, Elihu's presentation begins in chapter 31 and goes through to Job 37. He not only had much to say, but as we will see he approached it from the side angle of being an observer who in his mind had developed a much better and more convincing presentation.

There is another perspective and that is God's perspective. It is heavenly and it encompasses what is eternal. In a sense this perspective was described in Job 39:27-29, "Doth the eagle mount up at thy command, and make her nest on high? She dwelleth and abideth on the rock, upon the crag of the rock, and the strong place. From thence she seeketh the prey, *and* her eyes behold afar off."

From the height of heaven, God sees all things, and from the premise of eternity, He knows all things. He knows the past, the present, and the future, and He lines all matters up to His eternal plan of redemption. Nothing is too big or too small for Him to consider or use to bring about His will in light of His plan.

It is important to understand the heavenly perspective, but before we do, the first thing we must note is that there is no indication that the four companions in Job sought this perspective. Job's three friends assumed they knew God well enough that they could conclude that He is just and will only respond in such a matter when sin is found in the person; therefore, it all rested at

Job's feet. Elihu, on the other hand, thought that, "My words *shall be of* the uprightness of my heart: and my lips shall utter knowledge clearly" (Job 33:3). As you can see Job's friends **assumed** that they understood the matter at hand, while in the case of Elihu, he **presumed** that he knew what was going on.

I want to remind the reader, once again, God made it clear that Job's friends were wrong. After all, they had personal knowledge of Job, but chose to ignore the facts in order to confirm their conclusions, while Elihu's presumption was solely based on what he saw and thought he heard.

It is important to point out that assuming something will often make you look foolish in the end because you do not have all the facts, but presuming something makes you look like a fool because, not only are you void of the facts, but you are not open to be challenged or proven wrong.[4]

Now let us consider God's perspective.

---

[4] 2 Peter 2:10

4

Sovereign

*Difficulties afford a platform upon which He
can show Himself. Without them we would
never know how tender, faithful,
and almighty our God is.
(Hudson Taylor)*

We must understand that Job's four companions saw themselves as defending God's character. They felt that in light of the circumstances, if Job's character didn't have some hidden iniquity, that God would be the one whose reputation was on the line. After all, a just God would not allow such terrible things to happen to a righteous person. We can see this in the case of Elihu in Job 32:2, "Then was kindled the wrath of Elihu the son of Barachel the Buzite, of the kindred of Ram: against Job was his wrath kindled, because he justified himself rather than God."

The crux of the debate was not a matter of God's justice, but it was the trial of one man's faith. In the mind of the four companions, it was clearly God's reputation that was on the line. Again, this reminds us of perspective. The companions' perspectives were very limited, but God was seeing the whole spectrum of what was going on.

It is important to understand that these men's understanding of God was not wrong; rather, they were wrong about what was really going on. They didn't understand that God's reputation was not on the line because He was not behind this great testing of Job's faith. It is true He allowed it to happen, but as all-knowing

He knew something that Satan did not know—that Job's faith would endure the great test. Job would come out clinging to what He knew was true about his God in spite of the grave circumstances.

Again, we must remember that man's understanding is very limited. He only knows in part, sees in part, and has a very limited premise to operate from and within. It is true man thinks more highly of himself than he should, but every great testing of man's faith will knock him off of any pinnacle and bring him crashing down into the harsh reality that there are indeed mysteries that surround God that will remain unknown no matter how much man may seek God to understand.[1]

God as God reserves the right to keep some things hidden from man, while telling him exactly what he needs to know to finish the course. Deuteronomy 29:29 confirms this, "The secret *things belong* unto the LORD our God: but those *things which are* revealed *belong* unto us and to our children for ever, that *we* may do all the words of this law."

It is important to point out that **God will never explain Himself, but He will reveal Himself.** This simple truth is very important to grasp because this is what He does in Job. God never explained that the real culprit behind Job's plight was Satan and that what Satan was after was Job's faith. However, God does reveal Himself, especially to Job. Job said as much in Job 42:5, "I have heard of thee by the hearing of the ear: but now mine eye seeth thee."

Even though man stands on what he knows about God, he will inevitably hit confusion when He encounters the unexplainable ways of God's sovereignty. At some of the most trying times in our life God will reserve the right to be God, to be silent and mysterious, ever reminding us that behind the mysteries

---

[1] Romans 12:3 1 Corinthians 13:9, 12

surrounding Him is His sovereignty. The righteous Job admits as much when he confessed in Job 42:2-3, "I know that thou canst do every *thing*, and *that* no thought can be withholden from thee. Who *is* he that hideth counsel without knowledge? Therefore have I uttered that I understood not; things too wonderful for me, which I knew not." We know God is sovereign but it is this one aspect of His attributes that can bring each of us to the brink of complete anger towards Him, or a place where we give way to unbelief, despair, or utter madness.

God's sovereignty marks His supremacy over all matters, and that is where the great confusion comes in. Man asks, "Why God, since you have supremacy over all matters are You allowing this to happen?" I can't tell you how many times that question has been formed in my mind in my initial years as a Christian and how many times I had people ask me the question in complete anger and despair during times of great atrocities. How can you look into a grieving person's eyes who has lost both children to a rare disease and answer such a question? How can you advise a friend as to what he or she can say or do when trying to minister to a friend who just lost his family of six in a terrible fire?

The answer is you can't. You must admit you don't know the answer and only God does. You know that even though the answer rests with Him alone, His reputation is never on the line at such times; rather, man's faith is. Will man choose to trust God in terrible dark times, knowing that He knows all things? Will he acknowledge that only God can meet him in such depths of sorrow and despair?

It is at such times you must acknowledge that when the mysteriousness of God plunges a person into such great depths of darkness and despair that God has reserved the place and right that He alone is the only answer a person can and must seek. He, in His greatness and glory, is beyond the unexplainable, the indescribable, and unimaginable.

You will find this is true when it comes to God revealing certain aspects of Himself. Consider the great mystery revealed in 1 Timothy 3:16, "And without controversy great is the mystery of godliness: God was manifest in the flesh, justified in the Spirit, seen of angels, preached unto the Gentiles, believed on in the world, received up into glory."

We are told that the revelation of Jesus Christ, who is fully God and fully Man, is no longer a matter of controversy because it is no longer a secret that was hidden in types, shadows, and patterns in the Old Testament. It has been fully revealed in Christ and God's Word lays it out as being so. However, this subject is a point of major controversy among many religious groups. But we must keep in mind the unveiling of such secrets is the sole work of heaven. The Father draws us to the great work of His Son, His Son invites us to partake of the living Waters that bring salvation, and the Holy Spirit reproves and reveals truths concerning Jesus to our spirits.[2] We are told in Ephesians 1:17-18,

> That the God of our Lord Jesus Christ, the Father of glory, may give unto you the spirit of wisdom and revelation in the knowledge of him: The eyes of your understanding being enlightened; that ye may know what is the hope of his calling, and what the riches of the glory of his inheritance in the saints.

Obviously, if such truths that are beyond our understanding are not manifested to our spirits by the Spirit of the Living God, they will remain far from us, shrouded in confusion and at times causing us to go into unbelief.

It is the mysterious aspects of God that remind us He is God. Man is always trying to understand and humanize God in order to be at peace with his understanding of Him, but real peace only

---

[2] Matthew 16:17; John 6:44; 7:37-39

can come when our faith lands on what we do **know** is true about God and not what we **intellectually understand** about Him.

Since God is sovereign, nothing can be done outside of His will. This is an important point because it is only as we accept His sovereignty in all matters that we can completely surrender our will to His will, trusting Him to work out the details of a matter according to His eternal plan.

It is for this reason that we need to understand that God's will operates in three ways. There is God's **permissive** will. Since man has a will of his own and often chooses to go his own way, God will permit it, but man's way carries some tough consequences. He will reap what he has sown in the flesh, and in that reaping some have been known to turn back to God in repentance.[3]

God permitted Satan to bring the great testing on Job while determining the boundaries. This is clearly brought out in in Job 1:12 and Job 2:6.

The next way in which God's will operates is according to His **providential** will. This happens when a person asks God to have His way. God will often use circumstances to line the person up in the way he or she should go to bring about His desired results. If a person starts out in God's permissive will and begins to see the error and consequences to his or her way and turns and cries out to God, He will begin to bring about His providential will that will lead the person out of the difficulty in line with what He wants to accomplish. Keep in mind, God never wastes a good crisis. This truth is brought out in Genesis 50:20 when Joseph was assuring his brothers that there were no ill feelings, "But as for you, ye thought evil against me; *but* God meant it unto good, to bring to pass, as *it is* this day, to save much people alive." It is the Lord's goal to bring good out of crises, and even though God was

---

[3] 2 Corinthians 2:6-8; Galatians 6:7-8; 1 Timothy 1:18-20

permitting Satan to bring such devastation upon Job, Job was firmly in God's providential will and would in the end endure the great testing and be blessed.

The final aspect of God's will is for all matters to be brought into line with His **perfect** will. Romans 12:1-2 lines out God's perfect will.

> I beseech you therefore, brethren, by the mercies of God, that ye present your bodies a living sacrifice, holy, acceptable unto God, *which is* your reasonable service. And be not conformed to this world: but be ye transformed by the renewing of your mind, that ye may prove what *is* that good, and acceptable, and perfect, will of God.

In order to do God's will you must consecrate your body, in other words you must offer up your whole life, to seek after the Lord in order to know His will. Your mind must be renewed by the Spirit and the Word to properly discern what is the good (moral) and acceptable works that are being wrought by faith, to come into the place of doing the perfect will of God.

Jesus made this statement in John 4:34, "My meat is to do the will of him that sent me, and to finish his work." We have the pure milk of doctrine that we are to taste and drink of and the sustaining bread of Jesus' life that we must daily partake of by faith, but it is clear, the will of God is the meat that can only be eaten by those who are coming to full age. Those who eat meat are able to properly discern both good and evil.[4]

Spiritual milk will heighten our taste buds and bread will sustain us, but we must develop the teeth to properly chew the Word of God as a means to discern what is God's will. To develop our spiritual teeth, we must obey what we know is right up front. The truth is, we will not chew that which does not please our taste buds; therefore, we must develop a taste for the meat before we can properly chew it because it will prove contrary to the flesh.

---

[4] John 6:35; 1 Corinthians 3:1-3; Hebrews 5:11-14; 1 Peter 2:1-3

This brings us to the book of Job. For Job, the great debate came down to God's will. He knew God was sovereign; therefore, He was the One who permitted circumstances to come upon His people, but Job could not see how God's providential will fit into his present circumstance because it also appeared to be a matter of judgment which leads to separation and not necessarily perfection. In reality, it was all quite confusing to Job, but he knew and believed God enough that he would always come back to the fact that he would continue to trust Him even though nothing made sense.

In *The Companion Bible* the different names of God are distinguished in order to bring a proper understanding of how He approached His people and how His people approached Him. For example, the word "Lord" is presented two ways even in my KJV. When Lord is spelled, "LORD," it is in reference to Him being Jehovah (Yahweh) the covenant keeping God. When it is presented in normal fashion, "Lord," it is in relationship to Him being Adonai, the One who is our owner and blesses us.

Even in my KJV the word "God" is also presented in different ways. The regular presentation of the name "God" is "Elohim," our Creator. "Elohim" is used in relationship to all of His strength and power to bring all matters about, and is used 2700 times. When God is presented in all caps, "GOD," it points to Him being "El," which means "I AM He," divine, omnipotent, eternal, and ever present. In *The Companion Bible*, E. W. Bullinger distinguishes more of God's names in the Bible. One such name is, "Eloah." This name points to the One who deserves worship instead of idols, but it is also in relationship to God's **WILL** rather than His power.[5] It is clear that regardless of what is happening around man, man is within the sovereign working of God's will, but as to what aspect of God's will he is operating in comes down to his

---

[5] The Companion Bible Appendixes, pgs. 6, 7

personal will and the decisions he ultimately makes about his life and circumstances. While recognizing the sovereignty of God in all matters, the men in Job were struggling with the reason for God allowing such circumstances to happen to Job.

Another name that is used a certain way in Job that must be noted is "THE ALMIGHTY," "Shaddai," compared to Revelation 1:8, "the Almighty," was in relationship to carrying out all judgment. Being "The Almighty" clearly points to His power. However, in *The Companion's Bible* there is a distinction made in how this particular name is presented through the book of Job. When "The Almighty" is presented in all caps, it points not to His strength but to His **grace**, and not to Him as Creator, but as the **Giver**. This is to highlight that out of grace He is able to supply all the needs of His people.

The reason I am pointing this out is because the name, "Eloah" is used many times especially by Job.[6] It is also amazing that he and his companions used the term, "THE ALMIGHTY," along with "El," "GOD" throughout their debate. Most Christians are used to both names being combined in "El Shaddai."

It is natural to wrestle with God's will when we find ourselves in great spiritual darkness. God's will is a place, and to most of us, our thinking is if we are in His will we should be in the eye of the storm and not in the midst of the storm. However, being in the place of God's will sometimes bring the greatest darkness and storms our way. The consolation we can have while being in the center of the providential or perfect will of God is that regardless of what is barreling down on us, we are still in the safest place we can be and that in due time the winds will cease, the clouds will part, and the sun will once again shine on the terrain of our souls.

---

[6] Examples of "Eloah" used in Job according to *The Companion Bible*: Job 3:4,23; 4:9,17; 6:4,8-9; 9:13; 10:2; 11:5-7:12:4,6; 15:8;16:20; 19:6,21: 21:10, 19; 21:9,19; 22:12; 24:12; 27:3,8,10; 29:2,4; 31:2,6; 33:26

5

What Did They Know?

George Horne said that we on earth are
subject to threefold darkness—"the darkness
of error, the darkness of sorrow, the darkness
of death. To dispel these, God visited us by
His Word, with a threefold light—the light of
truth, the light of comfort, and the light of life."

One of the initial challenges I always had with the book of Job was the timeframe in which this great debate took place. I knew that Job was the oldest written book in the Bible and when I first read it, I felt like it was outside of the scope of time, and it was hard for me to put in context who these men were in light of the times they lived and the understanding they had about God.

I knew if I was going to understand who these men were, I had to have some type of scriptural reference point in which I could bring these men from outside of the vague notion that they simply existed into some historical premise that would put them in the midst of living souls who clearly walked this earth. This type of understanding would give me some semblance as to the culture that influenced them and their understanding of God.

I quickly discovered in my studies that there was one name that brought the book of Job into historical perspective. In a way this one name is like a neon sign in the barren wilderness of confusion. The man's is Eliphaz the Temanite. This name is found in the first book of the Bible in Genesis 36:15, "These *were* dukes of the sons of Esau: the sons of Eliphaz the firstborn *son* of Esau; duke Teman, duke Omar, duke Zepho, duke Kenaz"

The name "Eliphaz" is found in the lineage of Esau. This name means "God is his strength."[1] The Eliphaz in Job is associated with the duke of Teman, which made him a grandson of Esau. According to Jeremiah 49:7, wisdom had one time been associated with Teman. This means that Eliphaz would have been considered one of the wisemen of his people, but the important point is Eliphaz was a great grandson of Abraham. According to one of my most prized charts, there were only two years between the death of Noah and the birth of Abraham (2008 BC). Noah was 600 years old when the flood happened and lived another 350 years after the flood (2006 BC). On this same map it points out that Abraham lived 150 years during the life of Shem, Noah's son, and he no doubt received much understanding about the antediluvian time from his father and those of his generation.[2]

Abraham would have passed this information down to his son Isaac and Isaac to his two sons Esau and Jacob. Although some of the stories could almost have taken on a legend-like pose, they for the most part remained intact. The men in Job clearly understood who God was and the stories of their first parents as well as Noah and the ark.

The fact that much of their understanding in those days had come from their fathers was stipulated by Job. In Job 15:17-18 he stated, "I will shew thee, hear me; and that *which* I have seen I will declare; Which wise men have told from their fathers, and have not hid *it*:" In fact, much of the information they had was passed down from their fathers and perhaps they had received some of it from writings that were preserved by Noah.[3]

Abraham lived 175 years. He was 86 years old when Ishmael was born and 100 years old when Isaac was born. We know that Isaac was 40 years old when Rebekah became his wife. Jacob

---

[1] Smith's Bible Dictionary
[2] World History Chart in Accordance with Bible Chronology, © 2012
[3] Job 8:8-9

was 40 years old when he went to his uncle's place in Haran and spent 20 years there. We know this because Jacob's journey was tied into Esau taking his first two wives from the Canaanites.[4] If we consider when Eliphaz lived, it would have been within the period 1700 B.C. way into the 1600's B.C. because people still lived into their hundreds. My KJV guessed the day for Job's time to be 1520 BC, which would be during the period of Judges, but there was no mention of judges, Moses, Sinai, or the Torah by any of the men in the book of Job. Granted there are laws mentioned, but according the date that seems the most plausible to me was 1635 B.C. which was during the time of Joseph.[5]

If we conclude that the Eliphaz mentioned in Esau's lineage is the same one in Job, and we trace his timeline, this would mean he was closer to Joseph's time, and if we stay in line with this patriarch timeline, we can find some interesting names that are associated with some of the men that would have lived during the time of Joseph. For example, there is a Job mentioned in the genealogy of Jacob's sons who went into Egypt in Genesis 46. "And the sons of Issachar; Tola, and Phuvah, and **Job**, and Shimron" (Genesis 46:13). (Emphasis added.)

This is simply speculation because the Bible does not say whether the son of Issachar was also the Job of the book of Job. But there are a couple of interesting trivia points to highlight in the case of this Job. Besides living during the time of Eliphaz and being a great grandson of Abraham, the first trivia point is that this is the only other Job that is mentioned in Scripture besides the one in the book of Job. The second trivia point is that the descendants of Issachar were known to have, "understanding of the times to know what Israel ought to do" (1 Chronicles 12:32).

---

[4] Genesis 25:20,21; 26:34,35
[5] See *Tower of Babel,* © 2012 by Bodie Hodge, pgs. 253-263

The Job in the book of Job clearly had great understanding and insight.

Bildad is introduced as a Shuhite. We know that the word, "Shuhite" would identify him to a certain man by the name of Shuah and his family. It is amazing where we find a man named Shuah. He is a son of Abraham by Keturah.[6] If Bildad is from this man, it would mean that he was a grandson of Abraham as well and he could have lived during the time of Joseph.

We see for Eliphaz and Bildad that they could have been more than friends to Job. These men could have been relatives, but as for Zophar's origins, he can't be traced to a man, family, or town. Although "Naamathite," runs close to the name Naaman, which was a son of Benjamin in Genesis 46:21, the actual origin of the name, is "Naamah." [7]

As for Elihu, we know he was a son of Barachel the Buzite. They believe that "Buzite" found its origin in the name of "Buz" which was the second son of Milcah and Nahor, the brother of Abraham.[8] If Elihu was some great grandson of Nahor, he could have very well lived during the time of Joseph.

The only other information we have about this time period is that Job was of the land of Uz. We know that Issachar's son, Job, came with him to Egypt, but there is nothing that stated every member of the family stayed there. If this Job is the Job of the Bible, like his grandfather, Abraham, he could have been called out from land, kinsmen, and family for such a time, to establish his own witness of faith.

There is also speculation as to where this land was located, but because of the Sabeans and the Chaldeans being mentioned, Bible Scholars believe it is adjacent to their lands which would be north of the southern Arabians and west of the Euphrates and

---

[6] Genesis 25:1,2
[7] Smith's Bible Dictionary
[8] Ibid (See Genesis 22:20,21; Job 32:2)

adjacent to the Edomites of Mount Seir. The Edomites were descendants of Esau and build the famous city, Petra, which is located in modern day Jordan.[9]

Another important factor that needed to be in place for this debate to take place was language. The incident would have happened after the tower of Babel in Genesis 11, and these men would all have to speak the same language. There were 70 different languages that came forth out of Babel based on the descendants of Noah.[10] All five men had to speak a common language in order to understand each other. Abraham's language was Hebrew and was one of the Semitic languages.[11]

If 1635 B.C. was pretty close to the time this debate took place, these men would not be far removed from what happened in the Garden of Eden or the devastation of the great flood, for both were mentioned. Job 20:4 made this statement, "Knowest thou *not* this of old, since man was placed upon earth." This clearly points to the first parents in Eden.

Job is the one of the few individuals who gives us a clue into the character of Adam. We are told in Job 31:33, "If I covered my transgressions as Adam, by hiding mine iniquity in my bosom." It is clear that even though Adam was created in innocence, he was toying with matters that caused deviation in his character. Hosea referred to this moral deviation as being treacherous.[12]

In Job 22:15-18 we read this about the flood, "Hast thou marked the old way which wicked men have trodden? Which were cut down out of time, whose foundation was overflown with a flood: Which said unto God, Depart from us: and what can the Almighty do for them? Yet he filled their houses with good *things*:

---

[9] Smith's Bible Dictionary
[10] God Divided the Nations, © 1998 by Noah W. Hutchings, Hearthstone Publishing, ltd, pgs. 54, 55
[11] Ibid, pgs. 56, 57
[12] Hosea 6:7

but the counsel of the wicked is far from me." These verses show us that the Lord had filled the houses of the people before the flood with abundance, but due to their unappreciation of Him, they still told Him to depart from them.

These men knew about matters before the flood, but they also had much knowledge about God's creation. Keep in mind, Romans 1:20, declares that creation verifies there is a God, a Creator. The book of Job is considered one of the most scientific books in the Bible, and in this book, creation is clearly used to establish certain aspects of God's sovereignty and attributes. According to Henry M. Morris in his book, *The Remarkable Record of Job,* there are 15 or more scientific facts in this book, some that have been discovered 300 years ago and some more recently.[13]

One of the great debates of our time surrounds creation. To me it is amazing how some believe in the theory of evolution which finds it basis in humanism and is the religion of the atheists. The thought that men somehow came out of some swampy soup and evolved into apes who eventually graduated to backward cavemen is clearly disputed by the Bible as pointed out in the book of Job. This book makes it clear that man was put upon this earth. We know God created all things and that the unseen workings of creation verify this very fact.[14] To step outside of such a truth is to quickly slide into ignorance and paganism that will end up trying to explain creation from the premise of vain imagination and speculation.

What causes man to digress to a state of ignorance and paganism comes down to the fact he has chosen to drift away from his Creator and the record of truth He has given to all mankind. The two main factors that cause man to slide into such paganism is worldly knowledge and ignorance. Knowledge

---

[13] pg.35
[14] Romans 1:20

without wisdom puffs up and gives man a sense of infallibility, and ignorance causes him to bury himself into the tradition of superstition while swinging from limbs of wishful thinking.[15] The further man gets away from God and His truths and wisdom, the more he digresses spiritually, morally, mentally, and emotionally into a black pit of speculations, and the only way he will regain his senses, is to come back to his Creator.

Consider the times we live in. Just as Daniel prophesied in Daniel 12:4, knowledge has increased along with travel, but we have become like the days of Noah before the flood as brought out by Jesus Christ in Matthew 24:37-39. Regardless of our intellectual knowledge, our society has slid into such debauchery due to vain imaginations. The higher we establish the Babel's tower of knowledge by looking to the stars instead of to Him, the more man imagines that there is nothing he can't do if he puts his mind to it including reaching the heights of greatness and climbing over God's authority, but great his fall will prove to be in the end.[16]

When we study creation according to the Bible's presentation, ignorance, speculation, and error come crashing down in light of the evidence that backs up the obvious fact that all is a matter of intelligent design, the design of God our Creator. For example, the chance of life originating by natural processes on Planet Earth— is one in ten to the 40,000th power.[17] We know our planet is not millions of years old, but a relatively young planet. If we go by the equation of a day to God is a thousand years to us, we would have to conclude it is coming up to its 7,000-year mark, and there are aspects of creation that have confirmed that detail such as certain facts surrounding the sun.[18]

---

[15] 1 Corinthians 8:1,2
[16] Genesis 11:4-6; 2 Corinthians 10:3-5
[17] Footprints and the Stones of Time, Dr. Carl Baugh & Dr. Clifford Wilson, © 1992 by Dr. Carl Baugh, pg. 9
[18] 2 Peter 3:8

At one time it was believed that everything revolved around earth until 1543 A.D., but it revolves around the light source, the sun. Our sun is regarded as a G2 dwarf star or yellow star. Since the heat intensity of stars is divided into seven main classes based on the brightness that are emitted from them, our sun fits into the lower scale. For example, blue-white colored stars are considered the hottest and brightest stars which are followed by red-orange stars and down to white red stars which are the coolest.[19] The sun is the right size, located at the right distance from earth, and emits just the right amount of heat to keep life going on the planet. In the book "Footprints and the Stones of Time," Dr. Carl Baugh talked about how the sun is shrinking at five feet per hour.[20] If the earth was as old as the evolutionists have declared it to be, our sun would have long ago been burned out and none of us would be here to even have this discussion.

It was also believed that the earth was flat, a theory that could have been avoided if people would have believed what Isaiah 40:22 declared, "*It is* he that sitteth upon the circle of the earth, and the inhabitants thereof *are* as grasshoppers; that stretcheth out the heavens as a curtain, and spreadeth them out as a tent to dwell in." It is clear the earth is circular as proven by science and not flat like once believed by those operating in a dark age.

We spend so much money to prove there is other life in the vast universe while scientists observe the universe unfolding before them as pointed out by Isaiah 40:22, as well as Job 9:8. This Scripture talks about God spreading out the heavens. We logic since it is so vast, there must be life elsewhere and we debate about the need to locate it, but Isaiah 45:18 states, "For thus saith the LORD that created the heavens; God himself that formed the earth and made it; he hath established it, he created it

---

[19] Our Night Sky, Professor Edward M. Murphy, © 2010 by the Reaching Company, Published by the Great Courses.
[20] Ibid, pg.58

not in vain, he formed it to be inhabited: I *am* the LORD; and *there is* none else."

It is clear that God made earth a habitable planet for mankind. In the DVD and book, "The Privileged Planet," the authors proved that earth is the only real planet that could sustain complex life in the vast universe. There are different aspects of creation that must come together in the right measurement and function to ensure this complex life of mankind, animals and plant life, from light, location, tectonic activity, water, and the right atmosphere to name a few. As we will see, the book of Job discusses some of these functions.

I read an article in the monthly periodical "Prophecy in the News" some years back that pointed out scientists have discovered eleven dimensions. Clearly, each dimension is separated by space, time, and energy. For example, we use different calculations to try to put certain dimensions in perspective. We use inches, feet, and miles to calculate distances in our dimension, but we must graduate to light years away when we try to calculate the distances of the stars in the universe according to the speed of light. Beyond the measurement of light years is the astronomical unit. They use this unit to figure the distance between planets, only to end with the ultimate dimension of eternity where no measurement of time, space, and energy exists.

We are told in Genesis 1:2 that the earth at one time was without form, lying in darkness and void of any substance or life and that the Spirit of God moved upon the face of the earth. Job explained what the Spirit did in Job 26:13a, "By his spirit he hath garnished the heavens."

We know that the earth is part of a solar system that is located within the Milky Way Galaxy. This galaxy is a flat spiral galaxy and at the center of it is a black hole. It is estimated to have 200 to 400 billion stars. The earth is located in two distinct habitable zones, the *Circumstellar Habitable Zone* in the solar system and the *Galactic Habitable Zone* in the Milky Way Galaxy.[21] The truth is if the earth was five degrees off of its present course in the solar system in any direction, there would be no life.

In Job 9:6, it talks about the Lord shaking the earth out of her place and because of sin, we know that it groans under sin and one day will reel to and fro like a drunkard.[22] It is important to point out that up until recently the earth tilted anywhere from 22.1 to 24.5 degrees and that this tilt is what causes climate fluctuations, but there are some that have noted that it could be presently tilted even more because of what they have observed about the sun's position at such times as sunsets.[23]

Man has developed legends as to how earth maintains its place in the universe. Hindus believed the earth rested upon a turtle, which in turn rested upon the back of an elephant. The Greeks said the earth was held up upon the shoulders of the giant Atlas and the Egyptians thought it sat upon five great pillars. We have no idea how they explained what held up the elephant, the giant or the pillars, but the Bible explains it. Hebrews 11:3 states that the worlds were framed by the Word of God and Job 26:7 states, "He stretcheth out the north over the empty place, *and* hangeth the earth upon nothing," and Job 26:9 goes on to say that He holds back the face of His throne and spreads His cloud upon it.

On the third day, God created the greater light the sun and the lesser light the moon to establish time and seasons along with the stars to establish signs.[24] We have a large moon that is one-fourth the size of earth. The size of the moon is important because its

---

[21] The Privileged Planet, © 2004 by Guilermo Gonzalez and Jay W. Richards, Regnery Publishing, pgs.132-134, 152
[22] Isaiah 24:19,20; Romans 8:19-22
[23] The Privileged Planet, pg.4
[24] Genesis 1:13-18

gravitation pull is what keeps earth in its proper orbit and controls the climate changes and tides of the oceans. The planet earth is the only planet known to have eclipses which is possible because the moon is one quarter of the size of earth, and the sun is 400 times the size of the moon but it is also 400 times further away from the moon which allows for the phenomena of eclipses to take place. Obviously, such factors could only happen by design, not chance.

When it comes to the Milky Way, the earth, the blue planet which is a dot in the midst of the great Milky Way, is half way between the center of this galaxy, and is located between the arms of Perseus and Sagittarius. This position keeps it from being overrun with gases, safe from flying objects, and is in the right place to have a platform in which to observe the vastness of space. I believe God allows us to see the vastness of space to get a glimpse into His vastness.

Job 22:12 states that God resides in the height of the heaven and above the stars, and consider what Solomon said in 1 Kings 8:27, "But will God indeed dwell on the earth? behold, the heaven and heaven of heavens cannot contain thee; how much less this house that I have builded?" We are told in Job 38:31-33 that God alone knows the ordinance of heaven and has set the dominion of earth. It is amazing how insightful people like Job were during his time compared to people of later civilizations who worshipped creation such as the sun instead of the God and maker of the universe.

This brings us to the signs we have been given. God is clear that the heavenly lights were to serve as signs. According to the meaning of "signs" found in Strong's Exhaustive Concordance of the Bible, these signs were considered to be a signal, a flag, a beacon, monument, omen, evidence, or token.[25] We know that a

---

[25] #226

star guided the wise men to Jerusalem in search of the new king of Israel. Jesus rebuked the religious leaders because they could read the face of the sky but could not discern the signs of their times. They were seeking after signs, but all the signs that pointed to Jesus being their Messiah were ignored and rejected. Today, there are many signs happening around us, but some are false signs and wonders, especially in the sky. These false signs could be a matter of classified inventions, tricking the eyes with technology such as holograms, or it could be demonic activity, but they are preparing people to accept the antichrist who will gain loyalty by showing lying signs and wonders.[26]

The Witnesses

What do we need to understand about these heavenly signs? Job 38:19 makes reference to the way the light dwells and that darkness has its place. We know that light determines the places of darkness. We are told that the light of the world, Jesus penetrated the darkness of this age or world.[27]

Psalm 19:1-4 states this,

The heavens declare the glory of God; and the firmament sheweth his handywork. Day unto day uttereth speech, and night unto night sheweth knowledge. *There is* no speech nor language, *where* their voice is not heard. Their line is gone out through all the earth, and their words to the end of the world. In them hath he set a tabernacle for the sun."

The tabernacle for the sun points to the stars, and the formation we see in the sky every night remains in place.

[26] Genesis 1:14; Matthew 2:1,2;16:2-4; 2 Thessalonians 2:3-12
[27] John 1:4,5,9-11, 2 Corinthians 4:2-5

The sun moves through a path that astronomers call the "ecliptic," passing through what we know as the zodiac.[28] We see that all these signs serve as visible witness of God's glory and work. They are also sending forth a message, but what message? In the night they are giving us insight into some revelation and that the message they are sending will be seen and heard by all. Clearly, the message that is sent is a type of plumbline of truth that will go throughout the earth to the ends of the world.

We know that the Lord numbered the stars and named each of them. In fact, the Lord made it quite clear that he brought forth the Mazzaroth (Hebrew for zodiac). Job mentioned in Job 9:9 that God made Arcturus (branch and star in the constellation of Boötes), Orion (the brightest constellation that is associated with Taurus), Pleiades (a group of seven stars located in Taurus), and the chambers of the south. The Lord also made mention of Pleiades, Orion, and Arcturus, and Amos exhorted the Israelites to see Him who made the seven stars (Pleiades) and Orion in Amos 5:8.[29]

There are 12 signs in the sky (Virgo, Libra, Scorpio, Sagittarius, Capricornus, Aquarius, Pieces, Aries, Taurus, Cancer, and Leo), each associated with three constellations that some claim clearly tell a story. I realize that Satan has hijacked the zodiac and perverted the message that was established in the stars by the Creator. He has confused the message by making it mythical, occultic, or idolatrous and is using it as a means to foretell mankind's days and future. But as believers, we must remember who named the stars, the same names that are used today. This brings us back to just what message or truth are the stars sending forth that would cause the sun to sit in a type of moving tent for the world to see?

---

[28] Our Night Sky, pg. 34
[29] Job 38:31-32; Psalm 147:4

Although greatly debated, some believe that the stars are proclaiming the Gospel, the story of redemption. Keep in mind, that the story of redemption is foreshadowed in the Old Testament, revealed in the New Testament and serves as a thread that connects these two testaments together. Since this story of redemption is at the heart of God, why would He not use His signs to confirm it as well?

For example, the story of the stars begins with the virgin birth (Virgo) and ends with the Lion of the tribe of Judah's (Leo) victorious return as king to rule and reign. These 12 signs have been divided into three books that contain four chapters apiece that are marked by one of the signs. For example, in the first chapter of the first book we have the sign of Virgo beginning the first book and the first chapter. Virgo tells us the virgin birth of the desired one (the constellation Coma) who had dual natures (the constellation of Centaurus), but was pierced and offered up as an offering, and will come again (the constellation of Boötes). The name "Boötes," represented by a man with a branch that is called Arcturus, along with the brightest star with the same name in his left knee all mean the same thing, "He cometh." Jesus, as the Son of God and the Son of man, came the first time to become the Lamb of God and will come again as King, which is represented by the lion, Leo.[30]

To give you an example of how the story of redemption is presented in the signs and constellations, consider the table on the following pages. As you will see, whether you follow it down the columns or through each row, the story of redemption and His second coming are being presented in a powerful way.

---

[30] The Witness of the Stars by E. W. Bullinger (1837-1913), published by Kregel Publications, pg. 42

Chapters	1st Book	2nd Book	3rd Book
Theme of Each Book	The Redeemer Comes	The Redeemed: Redeemer's Suffering	Redeemer Comes Again
Chapter 1 (Theme)	*Promised Seed of Woman*	*The Blessings Procured*	*Messiah-the coming*
Sign: *Constellations:*	**Virgo (Virgin)** **Coma**-*The Desired* **Centaurus**-*Despised Sin Offering* **Boötes**-*Coming One*	**Capricornus** **Arrow**-*Sent* **Aquila**-*Smitten* **Delphinus**-*Dead One Rising*	**Taurus** **Orion**-*Breaking Forth* **Eridanus**-*Wrath Coming* **Auriga**-*Safety For the Redeemed*
Chapter 2 (Theme)	*Redeemer's Atoning Work*	*Blessings Ensured*	*Messiah's Reign*
Sign: *Constellations*	**Libra** **Crux**-*the Cross* **Lupus**-*Slain One* **Corona**-*Crown Bestowed*	**Aquarius** **Piscis Australis**-*Blessings Bestowed* **Pegasus**-*Blessings Coming Quickly* **Cygnus**-*Blesser Surely Returning*	**Gemini** **Lepus**-*Enemy Trodden Under* **Canis Major**-*Coming Prince* **Canis Minor**-*Exalted Redeemer*
Chapter 3 (Theme)	*Redeemer's Conflict*	*Blessing In Abeyance*	*Redeemed Possessions*
Sign: *Constellations*	**Scorpio** **Serpens**-Assault man's heel **Ophiuchus**-Man Grasping Serpent **Hercules**-Mighty Man Victorious	**Pisces** **The Band**-Great-Enemy (Cetus) Andromeda-Redeemed in Bondage **Cepheus**-Rescue Deliverer Coming	**Cancer** **Ursa Minor**-Lesser Sheepfold **Ursa Major**-Fold & Flock **Argo**-Pilgrims

			Arrive Home
Chapter 4 (Theme)	*The Redeemer Triumph*	*The Blessings Consummated and Enjoyed*	*Messiah's Triumph*
Sign: *Constellations*	**Sagittarius** **Lyra**-Praise Prepared for Conqueror **Ara**-Fire Prepared for Enemies **Draco**-Dragon Cast Down	**Aries** **Cassiopeia-The** Captive Delivered **Cetus**- Great Enemy Bound **Perseus**-The Breaker Delivering	**Leo** **Hydra**-Old Serpent Destroyed **Crater**-Cup of Wrath Poured Out **Corvus**-Birds of Prey Devouring

It is also important to talk about Pleiades. This word means, "the congregation of the judge or ruler."[31] It is a group of seven stars in the shoulder area of Taurus. There is a center star that is surrounded in a circular fashion by the remaining six stars. Some believe the center star could be the center of the universe, but it is also believed by some that these stars point to Jesus (center star) surrounded by His church, the congregation. When I learned about Pleiades, I was reminded of a Scripture in Isaiah 14:13 about Satan that puzzled me, "For thou hast said in thine heart, I will ascend into heaven, I will exalt my throne above the stars of God: I will sit also upon the mount of the congregation, in the sides of the north." As a church we are hid in Christ who is our place of refuge and strength, but Pleiades reminds us of Lucifer's desire to be exalted in such a way that he would be in the center of all things as well as judge and ruler over the Lord's congregation.

In Job 26:13, Job mentions that the Lord formed the crooked serpent. Who is the crooked serpent? As you can see from the

---

[31] Ibid, pg. 121

table, there are various representations of the symbol of Satan the serpent, which includes the three-headed snake, is found throughout the zodiac, but there are three constellations in relationship to the serpent's activities, and they are each located in the three sections that have been broken down in the story of redemption. The first one is called "Serpens," the second one "Drago," and the final one "Hydra." I heard that Drago is the longest constellation because of his crooked body extending through the Zodiac. In his book, *God the Master Mathematician,* Dr. Hutchings pointed out the 13th star in this constellation, a number which points to rebellion and apostasy, is positioned between the big and small dippers.[32] The big and small dippers are the hind quarters of the major and minor Ursa (the bear constellations). No doubt Job is making reference to this constellation. Drago's name in Greek means, "Trodden On."[33] As believers we have this promise in Romans 16:20, "And the God of peace shall bruise Satan under your feet shortly. The grace of our Lord Jesus Christ *be* with you. Amen."

Once again, I must remind the reader the presentation of the stars containing the Gospel is controversial, a matter that is sometimes very hotly debated. Whether one agrees in part as to its principle or completely as to its presentation, or disagrees with it altogether is a matter of personal conclusion and is a non-essential belief because it will not determine if one is saved or not. We also need to remind ourselves that missionaries learn the culture of other people so that they know how to show respect, but they also are looking for a key to unlock the people's understanding. It can be a legend or teaching that enables the light to come on so they can relate to Jesus and His redemption. After all, we need to see Jesus and as Paul stated when making

---

[32] pg. 93
[33] The Witness of the Stars, pg. 71

mention of those who preached Christ out of envy and strife to add to his affliction, "What then? notwithstanding, every way, whether in pretence, or in truth, Christ is preached; and I therein do rejoice, yea, and will rejoice"[34]

As you can see, I am just giving you a quick summary of the Gospel in the stars and if you are interested in finding out how such a conclusion was drawn, you can read about it in E. W. Bullinger's *The Companion Bible* appendix #12 or his book, *The Witness of the Stars,* and discern for yourself.

The Altar

As one studies the Bible from a scientific perspective, it reveals that our scientists are, at best, catching up to the workings of our universe and are simply confirming the validity of their own findings according to the Word of God. For example, Isaiah 40:12 tells us that dust of the earth is measured. We now know our planet weighs 6,000,000,000,000,000,000,000 tons and it makes 600,000,000 miles track around the sun at the amazing speed of 67,000 miles per hour.[35]

In his book, *The Puzzle of Ancient Man,* Donald Chittick wrote in the introduction that ancient artifacts reveal that there were electric batteries, sophisticated mechanical computing devices, machine-cut stones, and other items that show that man possessed a high level of technology even in the distant past. Clearly, in the mind of the evolutionist, such artifacts point to aliens not the intelligence of early man, but the Bible clearly brings out man's knowledge and capabilities.

In the antediluvian time we are given insight into the people's intelligence and capabilities. The descendants of Cain, such as

---

[34] Philippians 1:15-18
[35] Knothole Glimpses of Glory, F. Ellsworth Powell, pg. 227

Jabal, had knowledge of husbandry, and Jubal handled the harp and organ, while Zilah was the instructor of every artificer in brass and iron. There were musical instruments and means to extract brass and iron before the flood.[36]

Job talks about the vein of silver that needed to be mined, the dust of gold, the iron taken out of the earth, the brass that is molten out of the stone, and the fact that there are stones that are hidden in darkness and needed to be searched out. He was into husbandry, and his living and business most likely hinged on his herds, but he made reference to commercial trading in other areas when he made mention of the gold of Ophir, the coral and pearls, as well as the topaz of Ethiopia.[37]

The existence of these fore mentioned instruments, procedures, and materials throw doubt on the different ages establish by our scientists who put the Bronze Age at 2500-1200 B.C. and the Iron Age at 1200 B.C. onward.[38] The great intelligence that existed with the first men should not surprise us. Adam named every creature, names that we use today, and Cain, who was marked, was the first to establish a city.[39] Granted, he had to depart from God to do it, but it took great intelligence on his part to establish a functioning city. Noah built a great ark with gopher wood. The book, *Footprints and the Stones of Time,* points out that the gopher wood is not an actual species of wood but points to a process that is well-known today as the lamination process.[40]

Jeremiah 32:19 and 20 mentions the signs and wonders that have been set in the land of Egypt, while Isaiah 19:19-21 identifies it as an altar that sits in the midst of the land of Egypt. One might

---

[36] Genesis 4:20-22
[37] Job 28:1-3, 6, 16-19
[38] Halley's Bible Handbook, Henry H. Halley, 23rd edition © 1962, 24th edition © 1965, Zondervan Publishing House, pg. 70
[39] Genesis 2:19; 4:17
[40] pgs. 13-16

ask what this altar is. It is the Great Pyramid. In fact, it stands in the exact center of the landmass of the world and is regarded by some as the foundational stone of earth.[41]

It is believed that the Great Pyramid was built between 2900 B.C. and 2250 B.C., which means this incredible specimen of a structure was built around five centuries before the flood. In his book, *The Great Pyramid, Prophecy in Stone*, N. W. Hutchings shares how some ancients refer to it as the pillar of Enoch and as a result this godly man who is mentioned in Genesis 5:21-24 as walking with God, is also accredited as being the architect and possibly the builder of it.[42]

The construction of the pyramids still brings great wonder and challenge to those who are trying to unravel the logistics as to how mere man accomplished such a feat. For example, there are 30 theories as to the method that was used to construct the Great Pyramid. How did they manage to take an estimated 2.3 million blocks of stone that weigh in excess of 70 tons and put them in such a precise formation that they withstood the flood and still stand today as an incredible memorial to the genius of the designer and builder? How long would it take a workforce that could only work three months out of the year to build such a structure? The estimation in one case could not be more than two decades.[43]

Although we have the example of the Coral Castle in Miami Dade County, Florida, that was designed and constructed by one man, Edward Leedskalnin, these great structures remain a mystery. This castle shows us there are engineering means to move blocks weighing up to 30 tons with very little man power. It is speculated that in all the research Leeskalnin did at the local

---

[41] The Great Pyramid Prophecy in Stone, © 1996, 2010 by Noah Hutching, Defender Publishing, pg. 49
[42] pgs. 29-31, 54
[43] The Puzzle of Ancient Man, pgs. 127, 128

The Great Debate

library he might have studied the Biefield-Brown effect that demonstrates that there is a close relationship between electricity and gravity when moving great objects. Leedkalnin claimed he knew the secret of how the pyramids were built, but never left records or shared it with anyone.[44]

It would take another book, of which a few already exist, to explain the significance of the Great Pyramid, which includes depicting the Gospel of Jesus Christ. There is no question that the people before the flood had great knowledge and were far more advanced in their understanding than the Bible records and modern history acknowledges, but the witness is there for all to observe.

Many who study the writings of those who lived before the flood have discovered that, besides having hundreds of years to learn things, allowing their intelligence to hit great peaks, they also hit great depths of immorality. Writings before the flood have been discovered such as the Weld Prism and Nippur tablets that have distinguished ten major kings reigning before the flood. Granted, the length of their reigns was greatly exaggerated, but there is agreement that these renown kings existed, which brings us to another point of contention.[45]

There were also giants in the land and some perceive they were from one of those who ruled. Since these giants were referred to as, "sons of God," some believe they were descendants of fallen angels who mated with humans. In Job the title, Sons of God was given to angels, but according to my studies, the kings before the flood were considered "gods" and pretty well took whoever they desired for themselves and defiled and corrupted what was pure. It is also a known fact that some ancient cultures spoke of tall Caucasians that, after teaching them

[44] Ibid, pgs. 136-139
[45] Halley's Bible Handbook, pgs. 71, 72

64

wondrous truths, left, never to be heard from again. There are also skeletons of a giant race that have been discovered here in America and in other places of the world, but such discoveries have been kept quiet to control the narrative.[46]

Giants are not unusual and their remains prove to be very human. No doubt they carry a certain gene that has been passed down through generations, for the Bible speaks of their existence in the days of Israel and King David, and there are also those who live among us that are considered giants. Like many leaders who were considered "God" or a "god" of their times, the Nephilim race were probably of royalty and since power corrupts were simply evil giant men with insatiable appetites for greed and power. This would be more in line with what Scripture states about this subject. The Apostle Peter stated that God spared not the angels that sinned but cast them down to hell and delivered them into chains of darkness to be reserved unto judgment. The Apostle Paul talked about different flesh and different bodies and Jesus made this statement in relationship to marriage in heaven, "For in the resurrection they neither marry, nor are given in marriage, but are as the angels of God in heaven." Clearly, angels possess a different body than man on earth, and cannot reproduce after their kind.[47]

Man reached peaks of intellectual greatness, to only fall into moral debauchery and destruction, which can be seen throughout history by the ruins of great cities and mounds that now hide various civilizations built upon each other. In a tape I heard years ago, it stated that the educated men of the Medo-Persian empire were scientifically savvy enough that if it had not been conquered

---

[46] For more information on giants, see the books, *The Lost Worlds of Ancient America,* © 2012 by Frank Joseph, (chapter 39) and *Lost Cities of North & Central America,* © 1992 by David Hatcher Childress

[47] Numbers 13:33; Deuteronomy 2:10,11, 20, 3:11-13; Joshua 15:8; 17:15; 2 Samuel 21:16-22; 1 Chronicles 20:6-8; 1 Corinthians 15:39, 40; 2 Peter 2:4

by the Grecian empire who were, for the most part, into philosophy and not science, they would have been to the moon five hundred years before us. Oswald Chambers pointed out in the 1920 edition of his book, *Biblical Psychology,* that when the fifth century Greeks tried to explain the material world, they said that it was made of atoms, then it was discovered that you could split-up the elements that was referred to as molecules, and by splitting up the molecules they discovered electrons. Although there was some mix up with atoms and molecules, it was clear that the early atomist believed that the basic elements of reality were atoms— invisible and indestructible particles of matter which the Bible clearly makes reference to in Romans 1:20 when it states that the invisible things of creation confirms there is a God. Consider the great temples and statues of old, the great libraries such as the one burned in Alexandria by the Muslims, and the Romans with their form of government, roadways, and aqueducts, all which pointed to advanced civilizations, many which were brought down by what were considered to be "uncivilized barbarians."

This brings us back to what the men of Job knew. They knew quite a bit about God and His creation. Besides knowing about the stars, they knew the different cycles of the earth. In Job 14:18-10 and 26:11, these Scriptures make reference to earthquakes that take place along with the erosion of water that cuts through rocks. This book clearly makes reference to the hydrologic cycle that was rediscovered in recent years. This cycle describes the phrases which includes evaporation (ocean), atmospheric circulation (temperature and wind), condensation (storms), precipitation (rain), and run-off (snow) along with frozen ground and glaciers.[48] It makes reference to precise measurements and weights in this

---

[48] It is important to remember that the ice is like the paper and its layers are like the pens that mark time intervals as to changes in large climate swings that can occur over just a few years. (*The Privileged Planet*, pg. 41.)

process that proves amazing to those who first learn of it and incredible to those who study this cycle.[49]

Other interesting facts associated with Job surround the ice age. It is a known fact that we had one on earth and it had to happen before this incident took place in Job because the book mentions frozen ground and glaciers. In the book, *The Puzzle of Ancient Man,* the author explains in chapter six how the conditions of the flood set in motion the ice age, but it also points out how the early post-Flood dwellers possessed an amazing amount of accurate knowledge of the globe. The Piri Reis Map and other copies of very ancient maps, some discovered as recently as 100 years ago, show the entire coastline of Antarctica before the ice age. These maps have amazed many moderns. It is clear these pre-flood people were aware of the world's geography. Recent research, perhaps from dating the ice layers, indicates the ice age began within about 300 years after the flood.[50] Noah lived 350 years after the flood. This would mean that he witnessed the flood, the Tower of Babel, and the Ice Age in his lifetime. One would have to wonder if he might have thought to himself after the ice age, "What is this world coming to?"

The Fading Glory of Man

This chapter is simply touching the tip of the iceberg as to what is in the book of Job. Every time I approach it from a scientific level, I am overcome by what I've learned and discovered. This particular chapter is to inform the reader that the men who were involved in this debate were not uneducated, uninformed, or ignorant about the matters of God, of the universe around them, or about the tragic plight and spiritual challenges of humanity.

---

[49] Job 26:8-10, 12, 24-27; 37:16; 38:25-30
[50] Pgs. 58-59

Job came face to face with man's psychological process through suffering. We know that man is made up of body, soul, and spirit. Job understood that the soul of man can become bitter and the spirit of man can experience great anguish, but he also had an awareness of the physiology of man as well.[51]

Psalm 139:13-16 tells us God fearfully and wonderfully formed man. When a person studies such things as the cell, DNA, the makeup of the eye or ear, and the immune system, it becomes obvious that man's makeup speaks of a specimen that is wonderfully made, and that the presence of his spirit and soul reveals that he was meant to live forever.

Let us consider a few of these subjects. The cell which was thought to be simple has proven to be a magnificent miniature factory, a universe in and of itself where incredible amounts of information are read, processed, and replicated in every cell. We have over 30 trillion of these miniature universes in our bodies. If you spread these cells out, they would extend from the earth to the moon 100,000 times.

The DNA is part of the complex information processing system which is an advanced form of nanotechnology that mirrors and exceed our own invention in its complexity, storage, density, and logic. Although unseen by the naked eye, DNA could be stretched out to reach seven inches, but the incredible aspect of this thin strand is that it has enough information in it that it can fill 4,000 volumes. Since the information is being replicated in each cell, the volumes would fill the Grand Canyon 40 times.[52]

When you study the protein molecules that are involved in carrying out the information throughout each cell, one finds another aspect that declares that the working of our body is a

---

[51] Job 3:20; 7:11; 10:1,12; 12:10; 1 Thessalonians 5:23

[52] The information about the cells and DNA was obtained from the books, *Undeniable* by Douglas Axe and *Signature in the Cell* by Stephen C. Meyers, as well as the VHS, *Creation and the Bible*.

matter of intelligent design. These protein molecules are made up of a chain of different amino acids that must be read and copied in a different format that can be read by something called the ribosome. The ribosome will then put the right combination of amino acids in the right order to be transported by the RNA. There are 20 amino acids that can make up a possible 64 sequences that will comprise the chain. Apparently, a certain amino acid will even let the ribosome know when the protein chain is completed. Imagine, this is going on in every cell, 24/7 and it never skips a beat.

Sadly, something inserted itself into mankind bringing forth the curse of death upon that which was created to live forever, causing the tragic plight of man. We know what inserted itself into mankind: SIN. Man's life starts with such awe and wonderment, but ends in a coffin as depicted by the first book of Genesis.[53]

In Job 10:8-13 Job gives us insight into what they understood about the human body. He knew that man was formed from the dust of the earth, a clay vessel. He understood his inwards parts were outwardly clothed with skin and flesh as well as fenced in with bones and sinews. He recognized that life had been granted to him and that it was a matter of grace. It was also clear to him that the Lord had preserved his spirit and given him breath. These things he knew were true because they were in his heart as being so.

Job knew even though his flesh would perish, the spirit and breath that was given him were marked by eternity. He understood that man was born into a fallen, unclean condition, marked by a tragic ending, bringing him into subjection to some master. As Psalms and Peter declare, Job proclaimed man's body and strength are like a flower, here one day and gone the next. He recognized the end of humanity was the grave, but he also

---

[53] Genesis 50:24-26

possessed great hope, because as we will see, he believed in resurrection.[54]

The book of Job begins with a man, but for man to ensure a successful ending his story must end with God. Man may have been the last to be created, but he is and always will be the first priority of God. The book of Job summarizes the reality of man (his dependency on the unseen), the plight of man (sin), the struggle of man (faith), the development of man's character (sorrow) and the hope of man (God).

This once again brings us back to one man, Job and his journey to find the answer to that which seemed unfair, incomprehensible, and insane.

---

[54] Job 6:11; 7:6,7; 10:19,20; 14:1-4; 34:13-15; Psalm 103:14-16; 1 Peter 1:24

6

The Man Job

*Job is the type of man who could never rest in
the church, or in the scriptures, for he needs
living reality. The man who rests in creed
is apt to be a coward. The whole point of vital
Christianity is not the refusal to face things,
but a matter of personal relationship, and it
is the kind of thing that Job went through
which brings a man to this issue.*
(Oswald Chambers)

As a writer, I try to take note of how a book starts because in a sense it will set the tone of the rest of the book. Sometimes a book will begin with a certain historical fact, some type of introduction as to a certain person to set up an important event or establish authority as to what is about to be said, or to create a record.

The book of Job did not begin with an event, but with the actual character of a man named Job. Starting with the character of Job may seem a bit odd unless you understand that it would be the character of Job that would take center focus in the debate. The record of his character was clearly being established before readers found themselves being taken by the swift current of the debate.

Job was real and he lived in an actual place; therefore, the facts about him up front are not to be debated. Based on the calculation of God doubling everything for Job, and he lived 140 extra years after these events, he had to have been 70 years of age when he was met with the greatest trial of his life. In his time his age could have represented the prime of his life while heading towards the twilight of his years. For example, Abraham's father, Terah live to be 205 years old and Abraham 175 years.[1]

How can one honestly weigh the religion of man? James 1:26-27 gives us insight into what to consider and look for to see if a man is true to his religious convictions,

> If any man among you seem to be religious, and bridleth not his tongue, but deceiveth his own heart, this man's religion *is* vain. Pure religion and undefiled before God and the Father is this, To visit the fatherless and widows in their affliction, *and* to keep himself unspotted from the world."

The first test is the tongue. Did Job have control over this small member? We are told in Job 1:22 that Job did not charge God foolishly after losing his children and livelihood and in 2:10 that he did not sin with his lips after his health was attacked. Job even made reference to this very fact in Job 6:30 that he would discern if he tasted any iniquity in his tongue and would never curse even those who hated him. Job was willing to be properly instructed if his companions could prove their argument, while holding his tongue from giving an account or defense of what he knew to be true, but his companions could not provide any such evidence, and Job was not about to resort to a lie to get them off of his back.[2] He later went on to say in Job 27:4, "My lips shall not speak wickedness, nor my tongue utter deceit."

Job clearly passed the first test, but what about the second test? Being discreet in what you say may show wisdom, but religious convictions lack teeth, authority, and validity if they are not backed up with action, making one a hypocrite. In Job 29, he

---

[1] Genesis 11:32; 25:7; Job 6:24; 42:10-17
[2] Job 6:24-26; 31:30

gives a description of his actions before his ordeal. He delivered the poor, fatherless, and the vulnerable (stranger) in their plight. He had caused the widow's heart to sing and he was the eyes to the blind, the feet to the lame, and he comforted those who mourned.[3]

Job indeed passed the second test, but his companions perceived his defense to be nothing more than a cover up of some sin or a means to justify himself in his own sight to avoid accountability and repentance. No matter what Job said to push back their logic and arguments, they would not hear of it.

Keep in mind this test is found in James, but it was also part of the Law of Moses, and Ezekiel tells us that Sodom was not only destroyed because of it abominable sexual practices but because of pride, fulness of bread, abundance of idleness, and that the people didn't strengthen the hand of the poor and needy.[4] It begs the question—were there laws or codes that the people of Job's time lived according to?

Job does mention laws. These laws could have been what they refer to as the seven binding laws of Noah passed down to his descendants.[5] It is a list of seven "do nots" which include do not worship idols, curse God, murder, commit adultery, sexual immorality, theft, or eat flesh torn from an animal.

If Job lived during Joseph's time, like many people he might have also abided by Hammurabi's Code of Laws.[6] Hammurabi was a king of ancient Babylon and promoted the principle, an eye for an eye and a tooth for a tooth, and dealt with such matters as boundary disputes, but what I read of his laws, like Noah's laws they never addressed deceit, which might explain why Abraham and Isaac succumbed to such a practice.

---

[3] Job 29:12,13,15, 16, 25; 31:32
[4] Deuteronomy 10:19; 14:29; 24:17-21; 26:12,13; 27:19; Ezekiel 16:48-50
[5] Wiikepedia
[6] Halley's Bible Handbook, pg. 97

Job personally knew what was required of one whose religious practices were to be counted as being acceptable to God. He had to control his tongue and be a minister to the less fortunate, but did he keep himself unspotted from the world? Such separation would depend on his attitude towards God and sin, and as we will see, he had definite attitudes toward God and sin in place. However, he made some interesting statements in Job 31.

There are three portals that open man up to the corruption of the world: pride, the eyes, and the flesh. Pride takes man's mind captive, the flesh his lusts and affections, and the eyes his imagination. Job stated that he made a covenant with his eyes to not improperly look on a handmaiden and as a result he never allowed his heart to follow after his eye or be deceived by a woman. He stated that he did not make gold his hope or confidence, nor had he allowed his heart to secretly be enticed by idolatry. Another real indication of his attitude is found in the fact that he continually stood in the gap on behalf of his children. He sanctified them (type of separation) and offered sacrifices according to their number just in case they sinned or cursed God in their hearts.[7]

The later action reveals him as a mediator, a type of priest to his family. The word "daysman" was used in Job 9:33 in relationship to a mediator. Job admitted that there was no daysman to settle the dispute that was clearly taking center stage in the debate.

Job's religious convictions were real and he lived them out to the point that he was well-respected and looked up to by his community, which is brought out in Job 29:19-25. In spite of the accusations leveled at Job by his companions, the record is clear that this man had impeccable character, and to verify this

---

[7] Job 1:5; 31:1, 7,9, 24, 27; 1 John 2:15-17

declaration, the Lord confirmed the same testimony that was given in Job 1:1 in Job 1:8 and 2:3.

The reason the book of Job begins with his character is because it was thoroughly tested in the book and it would endure the test to the end. We are reminded in James of the patience of Job. In his affliction, Job decided to endure his suffering with patience, trusting in the end that he would experience God's pity and tender mercy, and when he was being accused by his companions, he proved longsuffering with them, trusting that the Lord would vindicate him.[8]

Patience (longsuffering) is one of the ingredients of the fruit of the Spirit, and Paul tells us that due to faith, we glory in tribulation knowing that it works patience, and patience because such experience finds its expectation in hope that is founded in the love of God. We cannot know patience without affliction. We can't choose the way of patience unless our character is being tested as we remain under the control of the Holy Spirit to ensure temperance of our attitude, longsuffering in our responses, and compassion in our reactions. Good, enduring character is forged in the ovens of affliction and is refined in times of testing. It is for this reason we are instructed to possess our souls in patience.[9]

It was clear that God had a man that He could point out as being perfect, upright, one that feared Him, and hated evil. These four facts were not only confirmed by God, but as already pointed out, were upheld by Job in the great debate.

It is important to determine the depth of Job's character before delving into the debate. We must remember that it was his character that was clearly on the line. The four companions perceived that the key to Job's plight came down to something being amiss in his character. In their struggle to confirm their own

---

[8] James 5:10,11
[9] Luke 21:19; Romans 5:2-5; Galatians 5:22-25

conclusions, Job's companions had to go into speculation about what Job did that would serve as acceptable evidence for their case. In their rush to confirm their own biased conclusions they ended up falsely accusing him and slandering his character. We know that the motivation behind such false accusation and slandering finds its source in Satan, the father of lies and the great accuser of the brethren.[10]

Before we consider Job's character based on what the Lord confirmed twice, we need to understand what defines real character. The book of Job even answers that question in Job 2:3,

> And the LORD said unto Satan, Hast thou considered my servant Job, that *there is* none like him in the earth, a perfect and an upright man, one that feareth God, and escheweth evil? and still he holdeth fast his integrity, although thou movedst me against him, to destroy him without cause."

The word I want you to note in this Scripture is "**integrity**.

According to the Strong Exhaustive Concordance, the word, "integrity" in the King James Version is mentioned only 16 times in the Old Testament, and none in the New Testament. Twice this word was found in reference to Abimelech rebuking Abraham for lying about Sarah and it was because of the leader's integrity that he was honorable towards Sarah and God withheld him from sinning. It is mentioned in 1 Kings 9:4 in relationship to King David, six times in Psalms, three times in Proverbs, and the remaining four references are found in Job.[11]

Clearly, this is not a word to be used lightly. According to the Strong's Concordance words such as "completeness," "innocence," "perfect," and "uprightness" are associated with this word.[12] Consider the first couple of words describing Job, "perfect"

[10] John 8:44
[11] Genesis 20:5,6
[12] #8537

and "uprightness." Are they not found in the words that are associated with integrity? The truth is that a person with integrity is going to be found innocent when it comes to motives, upright when it comes to intentions, possesses an honorable attitude towards God, His Word and ways, and hates sin because of what it does to God, souls, relationships, and testimonies.

Job's inner integrity is what kept him on the straight and narrow path of faith. Integrity will never let you betray your moral compass, sacrifice godly principles, and conveniently cast aside what you know to be true. In integrity there is no inner debate or conflict as to what you could do, because you already know what needs to be done.

I have met few people with integrity. They are like an oasis in the desert that refreshes your soul, a precious gem that adds great value to your life, and a gift that keeps on giving that which is excellent regardless of what else is going on.

It is important to point out who recognized the integrity of Job. First, the Lord recognized it. Remember what He pointed out to Satan in Job 2:3, that he still held fast to his integrity in spite of everything happening. It is important to point out in this Scripture that God also made it clear that what was happening to Job was brought on him without a cause or for some reason.[13] We must take note of this important acknowledgement because the main argument made by Job's four companions was that there was cause for God to bring this mayhem upon him.

The next person who recognized his integrity was his wife in Job 2:9, "Then said his wife unto him, Dost thou still retain thine integrity? curse God, and die." This woman lived with him and clearly recognized he was no hypocrite. This is a great confirmation as to the fact Job was consistent in his character regardless of who surrounded him and what he was doing.

---

[13] See Strong's Exhaustive Concordance as to the definition of "cause," in #2600.

I must at this point come to the defense of Job's wife. Even though her reaction was only mentioned once, people become very critical about her, but I have tried to put myself in her place. She had lost all of her children, along with their livelihood and now she was watching her husband suffer. How much crueler could life become to her? No doubt she was in a place of great emotional sorrow and mental distress. Clearly, depression was her sanctuary, great loss her bitter food, sorrow her tormenting companion, and hopelessness an anchor weighing down her sick soul. Her statement was, in all likelihood, the product of her state of mind, not her heart. It is important to note how Job responded. His response was to clearly give her a reality check as a means to push back the bitterness. He called her a foolish woman for speaking in such a manner but he never condemned her.[14]

The last two mentions of his integrity came from Job. It is interesting to see the context in which he mentions his integrity. In Job 27:5 he made this statement, "God forbid that I should justify you: till I die I will not remove mine integrity from me." This is a very telling statement. Job understood what his companions were trying to do. They were trying to coerce him into seeing it their way so they could become justified in their own sight. These men had falsely accused him, misjudged, and dishonored him and they wanted him to agree with them. The tendency for some people is to agree with those who are falsely accusing them just to get them off their back, but to Job that would mean he would have to compromise his integrity to do so, and he would not agree to such a false way.[15]

Job's final statement about his integrity is found in Job 31:6, "Let me be weighed in an even balance, that God may know mine integrity." Job had a boldness before the Lord because he knew

---

[14] Job 2:10
[15] Psalm 119:104, 128

the sum of his spiritual life and was not fearful of God weighing out his character. He knew that, unlike his companions, God would be just in His judgment of him. He had confidence because he knew who he was and the type of man his integrity had made him to be. After all, his integrity would not allow him to offer anything but the best, nor would it fail to choose the excellent ways which would ensure the fruits of righteousness. Job also understood something else, God's just judgments would eventually silence all false accusations leveled at him.

Let us now consider these four facts established about Job's integrity.

Perfect

Strong's Concordance uses words such as complete, pious, gentle, plain, and undefiled to describe one who is considered "perfect" in the Old Testament.[16] "Perfect" in this text is not being without fault; rather, it is a matter of possessing a right spirit that will bring balance and completion to one's attitude and conduct. It was God's spirit that made Adam a living soul and His Spirit that brings forth the new and abundant life in us. Although Jacob has been greatly criticized by biblical scholars through the years for pursuing his inheritance in a deceitful fashion, it is interesting to note that Jacob was considered a plain or perfect man according to Genesis 25:27. In other words, he possessed a right spirit towards the matters of God. This explained why he valued the birthright, while his fleshly, worldly brother, Esau, was willing to sell it for a bowl of pottage.[17]

Job made this statement in Job 27:3, "All the while my breath *is* in me, and the spirit of God *is* in my nostrils." Job

---

[16] #8535
[17] Genesis 2:7; 25:27-34; Hebrews 12:16,17

understood what spirit inspired and enabled him in his spiritual life. God clearly weighs the spirit in which we operate. The concept of spirit brings us back to our heart condition which determines our inward disposition When you study the word "perfect" in Scripture, it is associated with the heart.[18]

Remember how God pointed Job out to Satan, Psalm 37:37 tells us to mark the perfect man who no doubt serves as an example, a living witness that man can be perfect. God is looking for sincere devotion of heart towards what is right, a tender openness to what is good, and a purity that is present when receiving and handling matters of His kingdom. As Matthew 5:8 reminds us only the pure in heart will see the Lord and we know at the end of his ordeal, Job did see the Lord.[19]

God is always looking at the heart, testing its motives, exposing its intentions, and revealing whether it possesses His life or harbors the deadly ways of the flesh and the world. To have a pure motive means there are no self-serving agendas, no skipping along the surface to get by, and no half-hearted actions.

Job operated from the premise of purity in what he said and did. He declared that his prayer was pure even in his great trial.[20] Pure prayer is not about getting your way, but seeking God to come to terms with His way. In his struggles, Job sought the Lord. He made this statement in Job 16:20, "My friends scorn me: *but* mine eye poureth out *tears* unto God." God was Job's only defense against the accusations of his companions.

If you have a perfect heart towards the Lord you will also walk in a perfect way. This is important to point out. There will be no inconsistencies between what the perfect man declares and his

---

[18] Deuteronomy 8:2-6; 1 Samuel 16:7; I Kings 8:61; 2 Kings 20:3; Proverbs 16:2; Jeremiah 17:9,10; Matthew 15:15-19; Hebrews 4:12
[19] Job 42:5
[20] Job 16:17

walk. His walk verifies that he truly believes what he says and his words will give credence to his works.

Remember Job's wife acknowledged his integrity. Consider what Psalms 101:2 states, "I will behave myself wisely in a perfect way. O when wilt thou come unto me? I will walk within my house with a perfect heart." When you read Job's presentation of his life, he behaved himself wisely in his service to God and others, in public, and at home. Psalms 101:6 makes it clear that only those who faithfully walk in the perfect way are able to properly serve the Lord, and Proverbs 2:21 and 22 states that the upright shall dwell in the land and the perfect shall remain in it, but the wicked shall be cut off from the earth, and the transgressors shall be rooted out of it.

In the New Testament, the meaning of "perfect" is not much different from what was laid out in the Old Testament, however, it points to coming to full age, morally and mentally in relationship to inner growth.[21] This inner growth will manifest itself in works that brings our faith to perfection, spiritual agreement in spirit, honorable language, and godly love. Perfection finds its strength in the Lord and comes to assurance by resting and trusting in God's grace.[22]

James makes an important correlation between faith, patience, works, and perfection, "My brethren, count it all joy when ye fall into divers temptations; Knowing *this*, that the trying of your faith worketh patience, But let patience have *her* perfect work, that ye may be perfect and entire, wanting nothing" (James 1:2-4). It is the trying of our faith that works patience to endure, and as we will see Job's faith was tried to a point of complete destruction, but brought to a greater level of perfection through it. Consider what was said about Jesus in Hebrews 5:9, "And being made perfect,

---

[21] #5046

[22] Matthew 5:48; John 17:23; 2 Corinthians 12:9; 2 Timothy 3:17; James 3:2

he became the author of eternal salvation unto all them that obey him."

It is interesting to see how Job's perfection was addressed. Bildad made this statement in Job 8:20, "Behold, God will not cast away a perfect *man*, neither will he help the evil doers." In Bildad's mind Job's circumstances were evidence of God casting him away due to some unknown sin. However, Job's response to him in Job 9:20-22 was that if he tried to unfairly justify himself in some sin, that his perfection would prove to be perverse and that surely it would bring some conviction to his soul and he would despise his life due to hypocrisy. He goes on to say that he was aware that God can destroy both the perfect and wicked, but Job also knew that in the end the Lord would stand just in whatever He did.

Job recognized that if there was sin in him that the right spirit in him would bring conviction to his conscience, leanness to his spirit, and grave unrest to his soul until it was dealt with, but there was no such conviction, leanness, or unrest. His wrestling match was not with his life before the Lord, but with the darkness that had settled upon his soul that kept him from having clarity, hearing the voice of the Lord, and coming to a real place of peace in his spirit and rest in his soul.

Upright

Proverbs 11:3 states, "The integrity of the upright shall guide them: but the perverseness of transgressors shall destroy them," and Psalm 25:21 says, "Let integrity and uprightness preserve me; for I wait on thee." These two scriptures show that integrity and uprightness walk hand in hand. You can't be upright unless you have integrity and if you have integrity you will have that straight bent in your character that lines up to righteousness.

Uprightness pretty well defines itself. It means straight, something that proves to be well pleasing, and just.[23] My way to describe uprightness is **right standing in** God, **right being before** God, and **right doing in** obedience to God. Psalm 112:4 tells us this about the upright, "Unto the upright there ariseth light in the darkness: *he is* gracious, and full of compassion, and righteous." The light in the darkness mentioned in this Scripture is the Lord Himself.

Isaiah 33:15-16 gives us this promise,

> He that walketh righteously, and speaketh uprightly; he that despiseth the gain of oppressions, that shaketh his hands from holding of bribes, that stoppeth his ears from hearing of blood, and shutteth his eyes from seeing evil; He shall dwell on high: his place of defence *shall be* the munitions of rocks: bread shall be given him; his waters *shall be* sure.

We know to be upright you have to have an upright heart before God. Psalm 64:10 states, "The righteous shall be glad in the LORD, and shall trust in him; and all the upright in heart shall glory." Uprightness points to status, but one can't have right status before the Lord without a right heart condition. In 1 Kings 3:6, Solomon acknowledged that his father, King David had walked before the Lord in uprightness of heart. We are told that God beholds the upright, knows their days, will bless them with good things, save them, bestow upon them an everlasting inheritance, and that they will dwell not only in the land but in the Lord's presence forever.[24]

Upright status before the Lord also identifies him or her to a spiritual inheritance. Scriptures show that the upright are recipients of God's righteousness, and will naturally follow in the

---

[23] Strong's Exhaustive Concordance, #3477
[24] Psalm 7:10, 11:7; 32:11; 37:18; 112:2-4; 140:13; Proverbs 2:21; 28:10

way of righteous judgments. Isaiah 26:7 states the way of the just is uprightness and that the upright weighs the path of the just, and we are told that the righteousness of the perfect shall direct his way. Proverbs 10:29 tells us the Lord is what becomes the point of strength to the upright and as a result their way becomes a delight to Him. Scripture brings out the important fact that the upright are distinguished by the ways in which they walk in righteousness. King David asked this question in Psalm 15:1 and 2, "LORD, who shall abide in thy tabernacle? who shall dwell in thy holy hill? He that walketh uprightly, and worketh righteousness, and speaketh the truth in his heart." The upright have an assurance about their walk because they walk according to the ways of righteousness.[25]

There is so much in Scripture concerning uprightness. It already has been pointed out how Job spoke of his upright status when he made reference to his obedience to do right in regard to others. Job refused to walk in vanity which would hasten deceit, and he clearly stated that his righteousness would hold him fast and that in the end his heart would not bring any reproach against him.[26] He also made this statement in Job 29:14, "I put on righteousness, and it clothed me: my judgment *was* as a robe and a diadem." Righteousness was his garment, but righteous judgment was his royal robe and crown. How important is it to possess the ability to judge from the premise of righteousness? Jesus exhorted followers in John 7:24, to judge not according to appearance, but righteous judgment.

Job was not the only man who noted his righteous status. Eliphaz made reference to his righteous ways in Job 4:3 and 4, and the prophet Ezekiel also noted Job's righteousness four times in Ezekiel 14:14, 16, 18, and 20. Let's just take Ezekiel 14:14,

---

[25] Proverbs 10:9; 11:5, 20;15:21;
[26] Job 27:6; 31:5

"Though these three men, Noah, Daniel, and Job, were in it, they should deliver *but* their own souls by their righteousness, saith the Lord GOD."

My question is, why are these three men used as an example? Ezekiel made this reference to these saints when God was about to bring His heavy hand of judgment down on Jerusalem. The judgment would be great, and the three examples to others as to who would escape it would be Noah, Daniel, and Job. After pondering and studying it, I concluded that these three men represented those who overcame the three enemies of the soul by their faith in obedience, leaving behind an incredible record. Noah overcome the world, Daniel the flesh, and Job Satan.

Satan came against Job but his faith held in spite of the severe testing he went through. One of the reasons his faith held is because he had a sure testimony of having right standing before the Lord and no matter how much Satan and his companions tried to rob him of it through harsh judgments, kill what he knew was true about God with accusations, and destroy the life that had been established in him with slander, but Job maintained his integrity.

Righteousness puts a target on the lives of saints for Satan to aim at, and it puts up a mirror to those who are unrighteous, sometimes bringing swift retribution. It is for this reason we are told many are the afflictions of the righteous.[27]

Job, whose name implies "persecution," was no exception. Not only did Satan come after him without a cause, but so did his companions with a vicious desperation. The one who blatantly came against Job's righteousness was Elihu. He perceived that Job was only righteous in his own eyes and challenged him to prove it according to his satisfaction. He accused Job of saying that his righteousness was greater than God's and also implied

---

[27] Psalm 31:18; 34:19-22

that if Job was righteous, the Lord would have not withdrawn His eyes from him.[28]

The faith Job had towards God held him and as a result, he would not let his righteousness go no matter how much he was bombarded by the vain, wicked speculations of others.[29]

Feared God

The Apostle Paul said of the fallen man who had become indifferent to God, that he did not fear Him. There are different types of fear. There is the natural fear that serves as a caution light to us about possible physical dangers or losses if we continue forward. There is the fear of consequences that manifests itself in worldly sorrow when faced with paying consequences, as well as the personal fears where one is afraid of not making the grade, and the final one is the fear of God that will result in what we call true repentance. A good example of those who feared the consequences more than God was King Saul, and even though Job feared God, he also experienced the third type of fear in his great time of testing, while Cornelius is a good example of a Gentile who feared God. [30]

The first two fears are motivated by self-preservation, while the third one is afraid of failing some personal test, and the fourth one is the fear of God, which is motivated by godly love, a deep abiding respect or reverential awe, and a sensitive, humble spirit. It is expressed in obedience to what is considered acceptable, good and perfect to the Lord.

Our natural fear is to cause us to pause and become aware and discreet about pending danger, but it must never stop us in

---

[28] Job 32:1,2; 35:2,7; 36:7
[29] Job 27:5, 6
[30] 1 Samuel 15:18-35; Job 3:25; Acts 10:1,2; Romans 3:18

the middle of the road where either we will be left behind by life or left paralyzed by some imaginative road block or pending accident. On the other hand, we must not be foolish and discard the possible dangers awaiting us.

Sadly, many people fear possible consequences when it comes to doing wrong, but inwardly resent the fact that they can't do what they want. At this point, it is not a matter of what is right and wrong or obedience, but a type of forced discipline that keeps them in order. I remember through my childhood and teenage years, I decided to avoid certain questionable actions because I knew that somehow my parents would find out and I would pay the consequences.

Another important fact about those who fear consequences is that due to resentment, they fail to learn important lessons that instill real character. The lawless people of different societies do not have this inward discipline because many of them have not paid just consequences for wrong attitudes, decisions, or actions during their formative years, thereby, becoming foolish. People who do not fear consequences do not properly recognize or respect those who can dispense consequences. One of the reasons people have become indifferent to God is because they lack this discipline, and like Esau, when they begin to pay the consequences, and are brought down into a puddle of self-pity because they are unable to find a place of repentance.[31]

Job clearly and properly feared God, but he also experienced the third type of fear.[32] How many people have feared facing some test, realizing that it would greatly affect their grade, their goals, and their future? This fear had nothing to do with Job's character or faith; rather, it was about enduring the test with his character and faith intact.

---

[31] 2 Corinthians 7:10; Hebrews 12:16,17
[32] Job 3:25

For the righteous man, he is not afraid of hell because he trusts God; he is not afraid of chastisement for he welcomes and embraces such discipline; and, he is not concerned about looking like a fool because Jesus became of no reputation in a world that hates His followers, but what he dreads is displeasing God.[33] The idea of failing the test of faith is so abhorrent to the righteous that it is overwhelming, even though they also know that because they are in the flesh, they are also prone to such failure.

Man, in his weakest times, is forced to face the harsh fact that there is no other way to get through the present reality without walking through the great darkness that is before him. During this time the individual fears failing the test before reaching the desired goal. Job had clearly passed the test up front, but it was not over with. He had to walk through the emotional and mental upheaval without any light or hope at the end of the tunnel, and he had to do it while being bombarded with accusations.

Hebrews 5:7 gives this insight about Jesus, "and was heard in that he feared." Did Jesus fear man's beatings, accusations, and rejection of Him? Did He fear His ordeal on the cross? The answer is no, and if there was any fear, it was the fact that He had to endure the cross to the end in His fragile humanity, separated from the Father as He turned His back to Him when Jesus was taking on the sin of the world. Jesus dared not fail no matter how weak He became in His humanity.[34] This type of test is not just a physical test, but an emotional and mental test.

The one thing a righteous man is honest about is the weakness and ineptness of his humanness to get it right, or endure to the end when the billows of sorrow are great upon his soul. It is easy to sit on the sidelines of judgment, but let the same afflictions hit the one on the sidelines and that person will come face to face

---

[33] 1 Corinthians 4:9; Philippians 2:6,7
[34] Isaiah 59:2

with the terrible reality that such a great affront is too hard for mere man to bear.

It was as man that Jesus became a man of sorrows. There are four types of sufferings that create a different environment in our soul and both Jesus and Job experienced them. There is physical suffering brought on by physical pain that causes a certain restlessness and desperation in our soul. Emotional suffering will produce overwhelming despair in a person while mental suffering produces unbearable anguish, and spiritual suffering causes deep sorrow as one becomes isolated. During this time, they often feel separated from God and others.

The great struggle in the soul at this point is to hold onto some type of hope while clinging to a frayed rope of expectation that is swinging over the abyss of insanity until the dark night passes. After all, without hope faith is rendered ineffective, frustration turns into anger that becomes depression within, creating unbelief that is turned outward as the pool of despondency becomes a quagmire of complacency. Eventually, the person is swallowed up by self-pity because it seems unfair and senseless.

When a person is in such deep depths of despair, it calls for others to show mercy, but for many mercy is a matter of feeling or looking good and it must prove to be convenient; but once such mercy no longer serves him or her, it becomes another thing altogether.[35] For example, mercy without grace becomes cruel, mercy without compassion becomes indifferent, mercy without patience becomes judgmental, and mercy without love becomes impatient and accusing.

After Job lost everything, his livelihood, children, health, and his reputation due to no fault of his own, he came face to face with his worse fear. We can be critical of Job admitting just how overwhelming the great test was proving to be to his character, his

---

[35] Matthew 9:13; Romans 12:15; 2 Corinthians 1:3-7

testimony, and his religion, but in all honesty, we would be just as overwhelmed, and how many of us would be taken down into the deepest pit by the consuming dark depression of it to never resurface again? How would Job stand without a reason for living; how could he handle it without any hope of deliverance in his present life what might he do to climb out of the pit without reputation and support to encourage him; and how would he rise up and fight another day without strength? He had lost it all except his wife, and she was in her own pit of utter despair.

The thought of standing before a holy God who would show great displeasure for personal attitudes, failures, and actions that would cause any shame on His part and bring a reproach to one's testimony, becomes repulsive and unacceptable to a righteous person. As a result, obedience does not come out of duty and necessity for the righteous person, but out of doing the right thing because God is worthy of that which is honorable and glorifying to Him. In fact, everything that comes out of a healthy fear of God becomes worship to God.[36]

The Bible, especially in the book of Psalms, shows the benefits of possessing this healthy fear. It tells us the fear of the Lord is clean, making it pure. His secret, heritage, goodness, eye, hope, and mercy are upon them that fear Him. The Lord encamps around them and salvation is near to them for He will deliver their soul from death and keep them alive in famine. He takes pleasure in them and desires to give them their desires and will bless them.[37]

Another important aspect of the fear of the Lord is that it is the beginning of wisdom.[38] One of my favorite definitions of wisdom, is knowledge put into practice. Knowledge without practice remains simply a notion or concept, but if it can be put into practice

---

[36] Psalms 5:7; 15:4
[37] Psalms 19:9; 22:23, 24; 25:14; 34:7; 61:5; 85:9; 115:13,14; 145:19: 147:11
[38] Psalms 111:10

and it works, it becomes a source of wisdom because true wisdom can't exist without the necessary experience of proving that something is true and it works.

Wisdom is active and shows great discretion in what it does and says. It is upheld by the Spirit of revelation, is discreet in decision making, will never be inconsistent with what it believes, or dishonorable in actions.[39]

We all know about Proverbs and James, both books of wisdom, but in Job you will find one of the longest parables written in the Bible. It goes from Job 26-29 and guess what the subject of it is: WISDOM.[40] Job speaks of the God of wisdom and that His wisdom can be observed in creation and that it was clearly present in the beginning of creation. He points out the wise ways of God that are just as well as the eternal aspect of wisdom that can't be corralled by man, space, or logic because it is beyond explanation.

Even though the wisdom verified that Job feared God, both his fear of God and his wisdom were questioned by his companions. Eliphaz asked him how he could faint in such a time if he was a man of faith who had strengthened others who had fallen, was considered righteous, and feared God? How could he be in such a struggle in his soul? As for Elihu, he basically told Job to be quiet and he would teach him wisdom because he considered Job's words to be foolish.[41]

Shunning Evil

One of the things I have constantly reiterated is, "When are we going to agree with God about sin?" Whether it is sin in our nation, churches, or ourselves, we need to take on God's attitude towards

---

[39] James 3:17
[40] Note Job 26:3; 27:1; 28:28; 29:1
[41] Job 4:3-6; 33:33; 34:35

it in order to properly respond to it. Granted, there are some sins that God hates that are hidden or serve as an affront against the soul, such as the arrogance of pride and causing discord among the brethren. There are others sins He loathes (abominations to Him) such as practices that are an offense against the spirit and moral fiber of what is honorable and considered sacred such sexual immorality and murder along with sins done by the tongue. There are also violations that trespass the sense of justice, which brings insecurity to one's mind, such as stealing.[42]

However, sin is sin to God. It breaks fellowship with Him and relationships with others. It rips at what is just, defies what is worthy of consideration, and ultimately demands just recompense. It mocks what is righteous, pushes the boundaries of what is honorable, and shows blatant disregard towards what is true.

It is for this reason we are told in Isaiah 1:18 that God wants to reason with us about our sin. It is His goal to show forgiveness towards us and cleanse us of its destructive residues in our lives, but we first must see the serious offense in what we are doing and seek His forgiveness and cleansing because it is repulsive to Him in His holiness; therefore, it needs to be repulsive to us.

Psalms 139:22 talks about hating our enemies with a perfect hatred, while Psalms 97:10 instructs those who love the Lord to hate evil. Psalms 119:113 tells us to hate vain thoughts and Psalms 119:104 and 128 every false way. Sin is clearly the enemy of our souls and it often takes a pure hatred for something to be indifferent to its enticements and temptations, but the word, "eschewed" is an interesting word. Hatred is a repulsive attitude we adopt towards something, but to eschew something points to the action one takes against it. For example, to "eschew" evil means to depart from it because it is grievous, to remove or shun

---

[42] Leviticus 18; Proverbs 6:16-19; 25:25-28

it, to decline in it, avoid it, put it down or lay it aside, and/or to revolt against it in all out resistance or to completely withdraw from it.[43]

The word "evil" is also interesting. "Evil" means adversary, afflictions, bad calamity, displeasure, distress, heavy hurt, and wretchedness.[44] Wickedness has to do with practices but evil has to do with the state a person finds him or herself in. This person may fall into this state or he or she may bring it on oneself due to wicked practices.

It is clear that "evilness" was trying to bury Job. Such a state was something he avoided in his personal life and had instructed others in the ways of righteousness so they could avoid it. He found himself in a state of bewilderment because such a wretched condition had enfolded him, but his practices did not warrant such calamity to befall him.

Job was clearly perplexed by his situation and his companions did not help him in any way to properly face his personal battle over it. In Job 30:26, he made this statement, "When I looked for good, then evil came *unto me*: and when I waited for light, there came darkness." His companions implied he had some secret sin that brought this calamity upon him. They were obliging enough to set up scenarios as to what that unknown sin would have been.

One of the biggest hidden culprits they suspected, which would have not only broadsided an unsuspecting Job, but would warrant the distress upon his life, was pride. Elihu made reference to this very point in Job 35:12-14, "There they cry, but none giveth answer, because of the pride of evil men. Surely God will not hear vanity, neither will the Almighty regard it. Although thou sayest thou shalt not see him, *yet* judgment *is* before him; therefore trust thou in him."

---

[43] Strong's Exhaustive Concordance, #5493
[44] Ibid, #7451, 7489 with 7462

In many ways these men's case against Job appeared logical and exquisite. They often put it in light of it being true for a third party, but Job knew they believed him to be the third party. Eliphaz based his case on the argument that no evil shall touch the righteous and Bildad pointed out that God will not help evil doers, implying that Job could not expect any real deliverance.[45]

Job, however, maintained his innocence by distinguishing the fact that he understood what constituted evil to the Lord. In Job 24:21 he made reference to the fact that evil becomes a temptation to the wicked to deal treacherously with the vulnerable, showing that he was holding tightly to what he already knew to be his upright status before the Lord. In Job 28:28 he spoke about wisdom that departs from evil pointing to his attitude of fearing God, and in Job 31:27-30 he made this statement,

> And my heart hath been secretly enticed, or my mouth
> hath kissed my hand: This also *were* an iniquity *to be*
> *punished by* the judge: for I should have denied the
> God *that is* above. If I rejoiced at the destruction of him
> that hated me, or lifted up myself when evil found
> him: Neither have I suffered my mouth to sin by wishing
> a curse to his soul.

Job was pointing out that his heart would not tolerate personal pride and hypocrisy, and that he was not guilty of harboring iniquity, nor had he denied God in any way. He also pointed out that he was not the type to rejoice over the destruction of his enemies or cursed them, and as a result Job was confident that in the end he would be rightfully judged.

The Apostle Peter also made mention of eschewing evil by clearly identifying that which would set up the right state in which godliness could truly reside in 1 Peter 3:8-12,

---

[45] Job 5:19; 8:20

Finally, *be ye* all of one mind, having compassion one of another, love as brethren, *be* pitiful, *be* courteous: Not rendering evil for evil, or railing for railing: but contrariwise blessing; knowing that ye are thereunto called, that ye should inherit a blessing. For he that will love life, and see good days, let him refrain his tongue from evil, and his lips that they speak no guile: Let him eschew evil, and do good; let him seek peace, and ensue it. For the eyes of the Lord *are* over the righteous, and his ears *are open* unto their prayers: but the face of the Lord *is* against them that do evil.

God's eyes are on the righteous who eschew evil and Peter's exhortation is clear, as believers we must not give way to evil, nor return it to those who operate from it; rather, we must eschew it while choosing to do good and seeking peace, knowing the Lord's eyes are on the righteous, and His ears ever open to their prayers.

Although Job would be accused of operating in some state unbecoming to God and abhorrent to his conscience, Job would maintain his innocence because he was a man of integrity. He had been gravely tested and he had ensured a right spirit, maintained an upright status, still dreaded displeasing God, and had a repulsion towards evil through it. He had kept his faith and testimony intact in a time of great loss of livelihood, family, health, and reputation. During each test, he had not sinned in his heart, allowed his vain imaginations to go into useless speculation, or sinned with his mouth, and regardless of the onslaught of accusations from his companions, he would not compromise what he knew to be true. After all, his integrity would not allow it.

7

The Judgments

*God doesn't lead us into the valley, however, to keep
us there. His purpose is to refine us in the valley
of delayed answers and then bring us forth into the
sunlight of maturity and fruitfulness...You
don't **go out** of the valley; you **grow out** of the valley.*
(Bob Sorge)

Satan was after Job's faith. The enemy of man's souls just didn't want to humiliate Job to reveal some hypocrisy, he wanted to destroy him to silence his witness to God and his testimony before others. From all indications he believed that if Job lost everything, he would turn on God and curse him. It is not that Satan didn't understand and know man, for he does.

In most cases, man has to see how something will benefit him before chasing after something. Jesus even mentioned the fact that many wouldn't have followed Him if He had not provided them with physical bread. However, Job was not just any man because he was a man who possessed genuine faith towards God. Satan was clearly after Job's faith because if he failed to endure the test to the end, it would mean that God was not considered worthy of Job's consideration outside of personal gain. Again, regardless of what we lose in this world, it is all worth it if we gain the Lord.[1]

There were three **sources** that leveled four judgments at Job, and there are three **ways** judgment is executed in people's lives.

---

[1] John 6:26; Philippians 3:7-8

There are trials that have to do with developing faith, chastisement that involves disciplines in order to correct attitude or actions, and wrath, that entails rage that will result in justice and vengeance.[2]

Judgment has to do with separation, and separation comes in three ways: water, fire, and testing. Water cleanses, fire purges, and testing refines. Job would feel the fires and know the testing, but the cleansing ways of water would be far from him. He would be clearly put in the crucible where his faith would feel the great intense fires of the ovens. In such times, faith is placed in extreme places of heat. Granted, there is always that separation of the dross from the real prized substance that will prove to be valuable in the end.[3]

Satan would target Job's faith by attacking his livelihood, his family, his health, and his reputation. The first judgment would clearly be in line with Satan's character. We are told in John 10:10 that the thief comes to rob, kill, and destroy. In John 8:44 he is referred to as a murderer and the father of lies, and in 2 Corinthians 2:11, Paul talked about the devices of the enemy that we must not be ignorant of, which would include lying, accusations, and slandering. As we will see, these devices were used against Job.

In Satan's first affront, he used the Sabeans to steal the oxen and asses while killing all of the servants except for the one who was left to tell Job what had happened.[4] We see the first thing to be touched was Job's livelihood within his community. He made his living in husbandry as a means to provide for his family. Our livelihoods give us the means to be independent of relying on others to provide us with our needs.

The second attack of Satan was carried out through the Chaldeans. They took his camels and killed his servants except

---

[2] 1 Thessalonians 1:10; Hebrews 12:5-11; 1 Peter 1:6-9
[3] 1 Peter 1:5-9
[4] Job 1:14,15

for the one who escaped to bring him the bad news. Camels were used for transportation. Since Job spoke of kingdoms trading different goods, I wonder if he was not also involved with some aspect of the international business of importing and exporting goods, and if he was, he also lost his business.[5]

To be a successful businessman at any level requires one to have good standing or reputation in the community. A good reputation in your affairs affords a certain amount of respect and clout in dealing with issues in the community. According to Job, we know he had that type of respect in the community before he was stripped of it after going through his grave ordeal.[6]

The third affront from Satan had to be the most gut wrenching to Job and that was the death of his children. I have heard many testimonies after some tornado or flood ripped through a community. Those who survived but lost all their worldly goods will openly confess that you can replace things but you can't replace family.

Job could replace things, but he could not replace his children. His children had been partying at the eldest brother's house when it happened. A great wind caused the house to collapse on them and kill all, but the one servant who escaped to bring the bad tidings.[7]

Since God doubled all that Job lost in his ordeal, we see according to Job 1:2 that he had seven sons and three daughters before they perished, and we are told he had another seven sons and three daughters in Job 42:13 after his ordeal. When you consider his livestock before they were taken from him, he had to have least 4,665 sheep, 2,000 camels, 333 yoke of oxen, and 333 she asses.[8]

---

[5] Job 1:17; 28:15-19
[6] Job 29:19-25
[7] Job 1:13, 18,19
[8] Job 42:10, 12-13

It is important to note that there was one type of animal missing when it came to Job's livestock being stolen by raiding marauders from other kingdoms. The reason I left this animal out until this point is that Job 1:16 implies another type of judgment took place. Consider where this judgment came from, "While he *was* yet speaking, there came also another, and said, The fire of God is fallen from heaven, and hath burned up the sheep, and the servants, and consumed them; and I only am escaped alone to tell thee."

This judgment fell between the attacks of the Sabeans and the Chaldeans and it came from heaven. It appeared that God sent His fire down on the sheep consuming all including all the servants except one. This puzzled me until I realized that sheep were one animal that was dedicated and offered up to God. It was clear Satan was going to take all Job had, and it was only correct for the Lord to rightfully accept His own offering on behalf of Job. This would be considered a burnt offering which points to consecration. If you consider such offerings as presented by Noah in Genesis 8:20-21, Manoah in Judges 13:13-21 and Elijah on Mount Carmel in 1 Kings 18, along with the fire on the altar of Burnt Offering in the tabernacle and temple, once a fire consumed an offering it showed the Lord's approval of it. It was either the smoke or the fragrance that went up from the consumed sacrifice that served as sweet savor to Him.

We know according to the actions of Job that he most likely dedicated all to the Lord, but what would prove well pleasing to the Lord would be Job's faith that would stand, withstand, and endure to the end.[9] This offering was an indication that not only would God accept Job's ultimate sacrifice, but He would be well pleased with it.

---

[9] Hebrews 11:6

99

The numbers of Job's flocks and herds give us some insight into Job's wealth, but no doubt Job would have considered himself a rich man if his children had survived, but they were taken as well. Children represent legacy and it was clear that Satan desires to kill any legacy of the righteous.[10] He does not want to leave one seed behind or one root to grow up through the destruction. Satan's attack on Job's livelihood and legacy had to be thorough to prove his point that Job's faith would only run as deep as God's blessings.

What was Job's reaction to the utter destruction of his livelihood, his standing in the community, and his seed,

> Then Job arose, and rent his mantle, and shaved his head, and fell down upon the ground, and worshipped, And said, Naked came I out of my mother's womb, and naked shall I return thither: the LORD gave, and the LORD hath taken away; blessed be the name of the LORD. In all this Job sinned not, nor charged God foolishly.[11]

What an incredible response. The problem with many people who get caught up with the debate in Job is that they seem to forget Job's responses. His responses reveal a man with a deep abiding faith. In the first response, he rent his mantle which revealed a man in mourning, and shaved his head. This pointed to a total abasement of Job where all is laid bare before the Lord as he falls before Him, and in spite of the despair and sorrow, worshipped Him.

Again, how would the Lord look at Job's worship, as a pleasing sacrifice? Job acknowledged that God is Sovereign over all, and is the Provider of all things, which is a matter of His grace. He also was clear that the Lord was also worthy of being honored

---

[10] Psalm 127:3-5; Revelation 12:1-11
[11] Job 1:20-22

regardless of the situation at hand. Job did not sin in his heart or foolishly charge God with the trouble that had consumed much of his life.

The third attack of Satan was on Job's health. It is important to point out that there is no real indication as to the exact timeframe this took place. We know the initial judgments took place in one day, but the period between his great loss and the attack on his health is not known but Job does give us this possible insight in Job 7:3, "So am I made to possess months of vanity, and wearisome nights are appointed to me." It appeared as there were months between the first appearance of Satan before the Lord and his second appearance before Him in Job 2:1-3 where the enemy of man's soul received permission to attack Job's health. We also know that there were seven days that his companions sat with him before anything was said.[12] We can see by Job's description in the debate that attitudes towards him in his community had also greatly changed.

Before the final frontal attack of Satan on Job, the Lord once again points Job out to Satan as a man who held fast to his integrity in spite of him trying to destroy him without a cause. However, Satan had one more card up his sleeve. No doubt the Lord was not surprised at Satan's next proposition, but God knew it would not matter because Job's faith would hold.

Satan told the Lord that all a man has he would give to save his life and that if the Lord allowed him to touch his body, Job would curse Him to His face. Hebrews 2:14 and 15 makes reference to man's fear of death. The Lord did not put any real stipulation on Satan the first time but the second time He told him that he could do as he wished to Job's health, but his life was to be spared.[13]

---

[12] Job 2:13
[13] Job 2:4-6

Health represents strength, which points to the ability to endure a matter. In the first judgments Job lost his livelihood and children, but he still had his strength to somehow start over, but when he was struck with sore boils from the sole of his feet to his crown, he was completely rendered useless. The only thing at this point that Job could do was sit down among ashes and use a potsherd to scrape his skin.[14]

It is hard to imagine the great physical suffering Job had to endure. Suffering is a lonely road that no one can walk with you. It is for this reason that many people who are suffering find themselves very much alone, bearing the grave battle, while maintaining some type of sanity in the midst of severe emotional and mental anguish that makes everything seem insane. We know that when Job's companions saw him, they didn't recognize him and they lifted up their voices and wept, while tearing their mantles and sprinkling dust on their heads. Job admitted that his acquaintances were estranged from him, his kinsfolk had failed him, his friends had forgotten him, the maids of his house counted him as a stranger in their sight, and the servants ignored his intreats.[15]

The skin is considered the largest organ of the body. I had two friends that experienced similar physical challenges as Job. In one incident my friend and co-laborer, Jeannette, broke out with boils, eczema, and rashes from about her nose to the soles of her feet due to allergies and much toxicity in her liver and body. The suffering she endured was beyond any human comprehension. There were times she wanted out of her skin as the itching was unbearable, the pain immeasurable, and the suffering was endless. At night she bled on her sheets because of itching that was so deep that it was unreachable, as well as wrestling with her

---

[14] Job 2:7-8
[15] Job 2:11,12; 19:13-16

will to even live because the battle to go on was so incredible. There were no real days for her, just one long night that never seemed like it would end. Job made mention of this very fact in Job 7:4, "When I lie down, I say, When shall I arise, and the night be gone? and I am full of tossings to and fro unto the dawning of the day."

She could hardly stand to wear clothes because they proved such a discomfort to her and would at times scream in the shower when the chemically treated water hit her raw, inflamed skin. Job in his state even wore sackcloth which was very uncomfortable to even healthy skin and admitted his face was foul from weeping and his eyelids reflected the shadow of death because there was no real rest to be found for his soul.[16]

People who did not understand Jeannette's physical plight avoided her for fear of some type of contamination or because of uncertainty as to what to say or do. Job stated his breath had become corrupt and proved strange to his wife. He also declared that he had become a byword to the people.[17]

My other friend's problem was the result of picking up parasites in a foreign country. The skin on her legs and arms reminded me of the looks and texture of armadillo skin, but it was always weeping as infection oozed out through the cracks and bits of blood marked the places she scratched. She could not sleep in a bed so she slept in a chair, and had to avoid showers. Her care required the joint efforts of her and her husband, for two hours every morning, to take great measures so she could feel she was among the living each day. You could literally follow her everywhere she went as she left a trail of flaking skin behind her. She wore as little clothing as she could even though it was wintertime, and she would sit with ice on her arms and legs to

---

[16] Job 16:15-16
[17] Job 17:6; 19:17

103

soothe the inflammation and itching. Job stated that, "My flesh is clothed with worms and clods of dust; my skin is broken, and become loathsome" (Job 7:5).

The one thing that was completely taken away from both women besides their quality of life was their strength. Everything they did took what little bit of strength they had to just fight through each day and survive the mocking tormenting darkness of night. In Job 30:17, he admitted that his bones had been pierced in the night season and his sinew had no rest. I remember my friend admitting that the only thing she had to do through her ordeal was live because everything else was taken care of by her husband and a few friends. Job asked if his strength was as stone and his flesh as brass.[18] The answer was that in his mortal body, strength was not set in stone nor was his flesh something that could endure and remain unmoved by noxious affronts, but due to his integrity and faith, when it came to his convictions about God, they could not be moved.

For both of my friends it took months to wade through the shadow of the valley of death as they faced their mortality while death nipped at their heels. Even years later after their ordeal, their bodies still remain touchy, their skin sensitive, and their strength unpredictable.

What was Job's response to this attack against his health? We know his wife told him to let go of his integrity and curse God so he could die, but his response in Job 2:10, was one of faith, not utter despair, "But he said unto her, Thou speakest as one of the foolish women speaketh. What? shall we receive good at the hand of God, and shall we not receive evil? In all this did not Job sin with his lips."

At this point, Job had no strength to get up and properly worship God, but he still could speak and we are clearly told that

---

[18] Job 6:12

Job did not sin with his lips. In other words, he did not curse God so he could die in his time of enormous suffering; rather, he chose to live even though it meant great suffering for an unknown amount of time.

When one is standing in such a tenuous place, where the spark of life is barely shining through the utter mental anguish of the thick blanket of suffering, it would be so easy to let go of that small spark just to escape it. My friend, Jeannette, witnessed that small light during her ordeal. One dark night when her suffering was quite intense, I remember walking by her bedroom and feeling a coldness come out of it which I recognized as a spirit of death.

At the same time, she saw that the light of her life was very small and flickering. She knew all she had to do was direct her last breath at the small flickering flame and the very light of her life would go out. But through the darkness of it all she chose life; the life God gave her regardless of the great darkness of adversity that was trying to consume her in utter hopelessness. It was also probably around the same time that I rebuked the spirit of death in the Name above all names, the most precious name of all, Jesus. At His name, the spirit of death first bowed and then fled. Instantly warmth came back into the room and Jeannette's breathing returned to normal.

Job held to his faith in God through each grave testing, but the testing was not completed. You would think that when a man is down, others would see no need to continue kicking him when he doesn't even have the strength to get up, but Satan does not play fair. This enemy of God is playing for keeps, and he had no intention of letting an opponent gain any opportunity, or means, to stand and fight another day.

The next attack came from his companions. They had come to mourn with him and comfort him, but instead they became Satan's tools where every possible device from lies, false accusations, and suppositions, to slanders were used to tear down the last hold he had on his faith towards God, his testimony of God, and his reason to simply believe: his integrity.[19]

Romans 12:15 and 16 tells us to rejoice with those who rejoice and weep with them that weep and to be of the same mind towards each other and not mind high things that would keep each of us from humbling ourselves and entering in to show compassion. In 2 Corinthians 1:3-7, the Apostle Paul tells us our God is a Father of mercies and of all comfort. As believers, we are comforted in our sorrows so that we can comfort others in theirs. In other words, true ministry entails consolation.

These companions set up an appointment to come and mourn with Job as a means to comfort him, but instead they built a case against him in their minds and as a result attacked his integrity in all matters by falsely accusing him of not being forthright. They also questioned the uprightness of his character by implying he hid some iniquity, along with the validity of the wisdom he possessed, and that his hatred for evil was a façade. In other words, they were inferring that Job was not what he seemed or claimed to be but that he was a hypocrite.

Job was completely misunderstood by his companions. This man did not have anything really left except his integrity and when he refused to let them rob him of it, they accused him of being prideful, unreasonable, living in denial, and wicked. Job was not standing in defense of his integrity because such a virtue never has to be defended; rather, he was standing on it in order to set the record straight to preserve what was precious to him: his faith towards God.

Job had some clear statements about his companions. He called them miserable comforters and that they were forgers of lies and physicians of no value, and if they would hold their peace, they would show more wisdom. He claimed he could not find one

---

[19] Job 2:11

wise man among them, and pointed out that they vexed his soul and broke him in pieces with their words. He asked for pity from them, but they scorned and mocked him and persecuted him as if they were his just judges. He told how they had reproached him, but they were not ashamed that they had made themselves strange to him. His sad declarations summarized just how fair-weather and surface these men considered their relationship with him. He stated that all of his inward friends abhorred him and they whom he loved have turned against him, but the grave claim of Job against them is that they spoke wickedly for God and talked deceitfully for Him, which is considered blasphemous.[20]

The rule of thumb is those who you think will be faithful as friends often prove treacherous, while those who are less likely to be helpful step into the arena to encourage you, and prove that they have both character and commitment to do so. Sometimes friends that you once considered to be truly gifts from God become a bitter pill to swallow, but in the case of the unlikely ones proving to be friends, they become a surprising gift from God that ultimately brings joy and comfort to the soul.

---

[20] Job 13:4,5, 8; 16:2, 20; 17:10; 19:2,3, 5, 19, 21, 22; 21:3

8

Opening the Door

*The purpose of the theological crises is
not to change your theology (although
that will happen) but to change you.
(Bob Sorge)*

How does a debate begin? Someone must open the door to it. Sadly, Job opened the door to the great debate by lamenting his plight. After all, his companions came to mourn with him so they could comfort him, and it would seem natural for him to talk about the great debate that was taking place in his own soul. However, there had been seven days of silence between the five of them before the door was opened, and during that time his companions were no doubt personally wrestling with the "whys" of his plight and were building scenarios in the courtroom of their minds enabling them to come to their personal conclusions.

It is important at this point to understand the premise which Job started from and the one that his companions approached him from. Job started from what some would consider the low point of philosophy, while his companions started from what they perceived to be the high point of theology. Job started with the harsh reality of his plight while his companions were weighing Job's circumstances in light of a righteous God.

Theology will always begin with God's response towards a matter. For example, sin requires God to judge it in some way to bring man to repentance. However, when man leans heavily on his creeds and weighs out circumstances according to those beliefs to explain that which is not clear, he fails to discern what is happening in the spiritual realm because he is operating from mere opinionated assumptions and not truth.

This was true for Job's companions. Even though Job's status had changed, the man Job had not. It was true that Job's faith was being tested, but Job would always come back to what he believed about God, and what he knew as being so about God's righteous character. Theology allows people to fit circumstances into their creeds to make a judgment call about what is going on, but those living with the harshness of reality will prove that theology is not always applicable or practical when it comes to the challenging matters of life. Theology is incapable of explaining how something is part of God's greater plan to bring about desired results.

When individuals such as Job are trying to wade through the harsh realities of life, personal limited boxes of theology will always fail them. These boxes may hold correct beliefs about God, but they become mere platitudes, lifeless judgmental poses, and unrealistic notions at times of great inner personal struggles when one's plight seems unjust, unexplainable, and remains in the unknown in spite of prayers and questions.

Theology can only speak to the intellectual understanding of the mind, while drowning out the sorrowful issues of the heart, proving incapable of soothing the anguished spirit, or quieting the torments of the soul. I have learned that theology can't answer questions when what we believe ceases to make sense in light of reality, nor can it explain and address it when a matter emotionally touches us, leaving us in mental anguish and astonished and confused because our creed is incapable of making sense out of an insane world. In fact, the Jobs learn quickly that if they do not let go of their personal theology and let God remain shrouded by His mysterious sovereign ways, they will become totally skeptical towards Him. As for others who try to reach the depths of the devastating struggles of life from the heights of theology, they will always rob the Jobs of the opportunity to honestly face the personal inner struggles of their own life without fear of being judged for being weak.

For the Jobs of any age to honestly confront the "whys" of a matter, they must first let go of what they understand about God to accept what is in order to wade through the emotional and mental fallouts. Knowing about God from a theological perspective serves as a type of stake that reminds us of what we are standing on when our creeds are being challenged by heretical presentations, but they can't answer the fundamental questions that begin with the "whys" of a matter that seem unfair to the conscience, senseless to the mind, and mocking towards everything we hold dear when it comes to faith towards God.

I have stated many times that our faith begins when our understanding about God and life ceases. At such times it is not a matter of what we know or even understand about God; rather, it comes down to choosing to trust in **who He is**. This trust involves trusting His unchanging character, and knowing that regardless of what is happening His ways will always prove to be righteous.

The question is what do we start from when God seems quiet? We must start from what is in order to end up with the right premise and attitude about something. This means we start with what is happening to us in order to face the heavy blanket of mental anguish that is burying us under mounds of hopelessness, while still wading through the emotional fallout in order to come to terms with our view of life. Author Jerry Sittser said it best, "The quickest way for anyone to reach the sun and the light of day is not to run west, chasing after the setting sun, but to head east, plunging into the darkness until one comes to the sunrise."

We must honestly face and lament what is in order to come back to the stake of what was as a means to come to terms with what can be. **We must avoid seeking the need to understand before we face a matter; rather, we must face a matter to be brought to a place of understanding.**

Job's spirit was overwhelmed because his life in God was being met with a wall of silence and his soul was weary with life and in great torment because he could find no comfort or hope. His search for the light of understanding eluded him leaving him confused. Job admitted that he would speak according to the anguish in his spirit and the bitterness that was present in his soul. He asked why should his spirit not be troubled and admitted that his soul was poured out on him and the days of affliction had taken hold of him. His wish was that he was hidden in the grave away from the wrath until an appointed time where he once again could live life.[1]

To find the reasons for his plight, like every righteous person, Job no doubt began to chase after the setting sun so his plight would not plunge him into utter darkness until he resolved the darkness of uncertainty that was quickly coming upon him. He probably turned over every rock that could possibly trip him up with some unknown sin, looked behind every bush to make sure there was not some cave that hid wrong motives and agendas, and checked out every shadow to make sure there were no grey areas of compromise that would put him in a vulnerable place with God. However, after turning over every possibility in his mind, looking behind every deed to check out the motive in which he conducted the affairs of his life, and addressed the shadows of twilight, God remained silent. There was no conviction of sin, no heavenly finger pointing out some discrepancy in his character, and no prompting of the Spirit to delve into greater darkness to uncover that which was hidden.

He could not understand the reason for his plight and no doubt the silence of the Lord caused him to aimlessly wander in the endless "whys" that, especially after being affronted by his companions, became louder and more tormenting in the echo chamber of his soul. It is at this point that man can give up and fling himself into a morbid darkness of self-pity, curse his Creator

---

[1] Job 7:11; 10:1; 14:13-14; 21:4; 30:16

and die in his misery, or he can face the darkness in hopes of seeing the light. To face the darkness, he must consider a matter from the point of his philosophy about life. This is necessary in order to wade through the emotional and mental aspects that are looming as unclimbable mountains before him.

Philosophy will never answer the pressing matters of life, but what it will do is bring man to the end of himself. Life is a teacher. To live life is to recognize its changing cycles that brings forth growth and maturity, to experience life is to see it as an adventure that will expose strengths and weaknesses as you dare yourself to face its various challenges, and to face the adversity of life is to understand the fading glory of man as his body gives way to the workings of death.

Job admitted that he was fashioned by a Creator and was nothing more than clay. He was clothed in skin and flesh, born of woman and had an appointed time on earth. He came forth like a flower that would be cut down. His question was simple if a man dies, wastes away, and gives up the ghost, where is he, and will he live again? Job would answer the question, but there is always that nagging notion that causes one to ask, "Is this all there is to life, the curse of it, ever producing the anguished spirit, the bitter soul of sorrow, and finally the grave?"[2]

When people face the mortality of life, they can't help but think about the end of man as far as this present life: the grave. Job mentioned the grave many times. There are different meanings of grave in Scripture, all of them used in the book of Job. According to Strong's Concordance, the meanings of "grave" are hades, world of death, hell, pit, sepulcher, a burying place, and a point of humility.[3]

There was one Scripture about the grave that caused me to pause. It is found in Job 30:24, "Howbeit he will not stretch out *his* hand to the grave, though they cry in his destruction." The

[2] Job 7:1; 10:8-12; 14:1-2,10-14
[3] Job 3:22; 7:9--10; 14:13; 17:1,13; 21:13, 33:22. (# 6913 & 7585)

idea of grave in this Scripture is associated with prayer, intercession, and request.[4] God will not stretch forth His hand and save us from the grave when our time comes, but as rebellious man faces his own mortality and the grave, he remains a fool who still sees no need for repentance and deliverance, even though there are those who care about his life and soul.

To face life for what it is, can cause one to come across morbid and accusing towards the One who is the giver and sustainer of all life. We see this with Job. He cursed the day he was born and made it clear that he wished he had never been born. He could not understand how he could be brought forth from the womb to only taste the bitterness of the soul. If only he had never taken the first breath, and if his mother would have resisted his birth, he would have been spared the fear he wanted to avoid in such adversity, and would be spared from the great anguish and sorrow that were consuming his soul.[5]

God is not going to fall off his throne as man wrestles with the issues of life that make no sense to his finite mind. Granted, for Job's companions his struggle to understand caused him to look unbelieving and foolish, his rejection to repent of some unknown sin made him look unreasonable and unteachable, and his defense of himself made him look arrogant. No matter how Job cut it, he looked as if he was hiding some sin, guilty of moral deviation, or operating from a wrong spirit.

However, he was also causing great unrest to his companions' souls. These companions could not reach the depths of where Job was wrestling with his own questions with their intellectual knowledge of God. In order to reach Job, they would have to recognize that their theology could not identify with Job and admit they, too, did not have any explanation, but they could encourage Job by reminding him that they still could bank on one truth, God is God. Job's resistance to agree with them in their conclusions,

---

[4] # 1164 also refer to #1158
[5] Job 3:1-4, 10-12, 20, 25

caused their theology to teeter and eventually fall off the pedestal, leaving their perception of God with a black eye, but for Job, what he knew about God was not only being confirmed, but clarified in greater measure.

God does not condemn man for asking the hard questions that often resonates in his heart when he faces the injustice of the curse that is upon all life due to sin. He does not condemn him from speaking from the anguish of his spirit and the bitterness of his soul because He knows his frame and desires to show pity. He knows at such times man is striving to climb over and above the devastating terrain of his soul to find the sanity behind a matter. As Job pointed out, man came with nothing into this world and will leave it in the same way.[6] The only thing man can take with him is his character and Job had integrity when it came to his faith. Since Job had faith, his search for the light led him to the end of himself.

It is at the end of self where true faith kicks in to bring the person to three sound conclusions: 1) there is a God, 2) I am not Him, and 3) nothing makes sense outside of God. At the end of man's wrestling match about the matters of God and life is a clear choice of faith. In fact, faith is the only clear choice in this match and it is who God is that man will come to rest on, knowing He is the immovable Rock that will never cease to be who He is, or move from what is true, or change with the times.

As it becomes obvious in the debate, Job honestly faced the darkness of his present situation and let it consume his theology about God while ultimately choosing to land on the runway of faith as he came to rest on the reality of who God is. The reality of this present life is fading, the reality of the world is temporary, but the reality of God is forever. Job would cling to the unseen reality of the eternal and in doing so would find strength, hope, comfort, and in the end vindication.

---

[6] Job 1:21; Psalm 103:10-18

9

The Dreamer
(Job 4-5)

*Theology is tested by history
and logic; religions must be
tested by experience.
(Oswald Chambers)*

Eliphaz is an interesting man. His name means "God is his strength."[1] This friend of Job approached him from a personal experience that he assumed was meant for his struggling friend since it brought confusion to him. In his mind it couldn't possibly be intended for him. It becomes obvious that Eliphaz tried to fit Job's circumstances into his theology by using his personal experience to verify his religious conclusion.

Eliphaz felt Job's plight cleared up the confusion that his experience had caused him, but in reality, it created a type of bias that would prove to become a point of prejudice and judgmentalism leveled at Job.

Eliphaz started from a diplomatic angle to communicate what he perceived was the case for Job, while acknowledging it would probably not be received. He also acknowledged that Job had instructed many and strengthened the weak. This showed that Eliphaz had a history with Job and had recognized that he was a man who upheld his religious convictions by his actions, but he

---

[1] Smith's Bible Dictionary

used Job's previous pious actions to basically ask him, "Where is your faith now?"[2]

Job was not showing a lack of faith, but wrestling with the state of his affairs. He talked about his great grief and the weight of it upon his soul and that he simply wanted to be delivered from it. He admitted that God's arrows were within him and that poison had penetrated his spirit, leaving him with what seemed bitter and hopeless, but that like any animal who was in affliction, he was making his distress known. Job simply asked why prolong his life if there was no strength to live it; after all, the essence of his strength and his hope seemed silent and far away. He confessed that if he knew when his suffering was coming to an end, he could find comfort in it.[3]

This was truly a statement of faith. Job was admitting it was the darkness of the unknown that caused the greatest distress. His suffering seemed endless, and if he only knew that there was a limit to it, he would harden himself against its despair and find comfort in it because it would be a trustworthy revelation from God. He did not want God to spare his life in such a state. His next words seem to possess a boldness that, in spite of his present life seemingly coming to an end, he had confidence that he would stand before the Lord in death, "for I have not concealed the words of the Holy One."[4]

This statement may not seem important, but it is an important insight into Job. Job believed God's Word, or teaching, to the extent that he lived it, taught it, and held onto it. Romans 10:17 tells us that faith comes by hearing and hearing by the Word of God. Clearly, it was not the suffering that was causing such distress for Job, it was God's silence. He just wanted to hear from Him. He wanted direction from heaven because it would revive his

---

[2] Job 4:2-6
[3] Job 6:1-13
[4] Job 6:10

strength and cause the expectation of hope to take flight once again.

There is another important point to bring out in Job's discourse in Job 6:13, "Is not my help in me? And is wisdom driven quite from me?" Job understood the breath of God, the Holy Spirit was within him, and that it is the Spirit of God that brings forth wisdom and revelation.[5] He may not have felt the presence of God, but he believed that the life of God was very much present.

Eliphaz's response reveals that he was not trying to identify with Job; rather, he felt a great need to reveal the folly of Job's attitude towards his plight and instruct him. He used Job's inner wrestling match to set up the precedent for his case against him. Clearly, if Job was an upright man, he would not be struggling with such matters. It was easy for Eliphaz to judge Job from a religious pose, but if the shoe was on the other foot, how would Eliphaz have responded?

Job made an interesting statement in response in Job 6:14, "To him that is afflicted pity should be shewed for his friend; but he forsaketh the fear of the Almighty." This statement is directed at Eliphaz. Eliphaz came as a friend to comfort Job, which would require him to show pity, but instead like other brethren, he was deceitfully dealing with him because his understanding was darkened, his heart had grown cold, and when tested it would be consumed by the heat. Job made it clear that the core of Eliphaz's problem was that he did not fear the Lord.[6]

Eliphaz eloquently set forth his case by pointing out that the innocent and righteous would not be allowed to perish and he then went on to present the case against those who will perish. The people marked for judgment are those who plow iniquity and sow wickedness, along with the prideful who will either be brought

---

[5] Job 27:3; Ephesians 1:17,
[6] Job 6:15-17

down in judgment or scattered, for the blast of God will cause them to perish and the breath of His nostrils will consume them.[7]

It is clear that Eliphaz saw Job's circumstances as being the response of a righteous God to some type of hidden sin in his life because he made reference to iniquity which is moral deviation. Iniquity is the unseen state of prideful, selfish man but sins associated with it can be plowed under and hidden away.[8] This is important to note because if Eliphaz was speaking on behalf of God, any hidden sin in Job's life would have been made known to Eliphaz because man can't repent of something that is vague or requires him to guess. The spirit in the righteous man such as Job would clearly be convicted if any such sin was exposed and would come quickly into agreement as a means to address it in repentance and humiliation.

Job challenged Eliphaz in his response to him by inviting him to teach him where he was wrong to bring proper understanding to him and he became silent. Job admitted that Eliphaz's words were forcible as in the sense of being passionate, but they lacked validity.[9]

This is where we come to Eliphaz's foundation that served as both his premise for his case and confirmation that there had to be some hidden sin in Job's life since it was evident in his mind that Job was perishing, not suffering. It was a dream. In Job 4:14-21, we are told this dream. Eliphaz describes his response towards it as fear coming on him, causing him to tremble and shake and then a spirit passed before his face and the hair stood up on his skin.

It is at this point that Eliphaz admits something very important, and that was he could not discern the form. We are told we must

---

[7] Job 4:7-9
[8] Job 4:7, 8
[9] Job 6:24-26

discern the spirit before we can come into any agreement with it.[10] There was some type of image before him and he heard a voice saying,

> Shall mortal man be more just than God? shall a man be more pure than his maker? Behold, he put no trust in his servants; and his angels he charged with folly: How much less *in* them that dwell in houses of clay, whose foundation *is* in the dust, *which* are crushed before the moth? They are destroyed from morning to evening: they perish for ever without any regarding *it*. Doth not their excellency *which is* in them go away? they die, even without wisdom.

The first thing we must note is that this spirit brought fear, trembling, and shaking on Eliphaz as his hair stood up on his skin. His response reveals that his experience was troubling enough that he would not forget it. Now we come to what was said. We first must discern if it was connected to Job in some way and then we must determine if it was directed at Eliphaz in relationship to ministering to Job or if it was given to Eliphaz to instruct Job.

I believe that the dream was a warning to Eliphaz to be careful of his attitude towards Job because he would be tested and fail to see, understand, and walk carefully before the Lord. He ended up foolishly transposing his dream onto Job. Eliphaz felt that Job's inner wrestling match about his plight and quality of life was a black eye to God, but what Eliphaz accredited to Job based on his dream had nothing to do with what Job was wrestling with. Eliphaz failed to understand that he was not sent to be judge and jury of Job because God clearly did not entrust him with the proper knowledge to be in any position other than one who was to comfort. After all, he was made of clay and dust and could easily be crushed because death works in each of us. We are always

---

[10] 1 Corinthians 2:12-14; 1 John 4:1

walking towards our demise and we can't take anything with us from this world. All we can leave behind is that which has the eternal mark of God on it.

As I consider Eliphaz, he is the one who thought highly enough of himself that he appointed himself as judge and jury over Job without seeking any real indictment from God. It was as if he was looking into some glass ball as a means to interpret his confusing dream to nobly take offense for God while trying to exalt his justice over Job, claiming his intentions were pure, but his folly as a servant was his blatant failure to properly discern the prideful spirit behind him. He may have seen himself as being wise, but in the end, he, not Job, was proven to be wrong and foolish.

I believe Job made reference to this dream when he asked him in Job 6:26, "Do ye imagine to reprove words?" What words needed to be reproved? God's Words stand and need no explanation or reproving. They need to be believed and applied correctly. Job stated that Eliphaz's speech was that of a desperate man, and his words were like the wind that may blow in with gusto but ceases to be. In other words, they never hit the mark or properly landed in the right place to plant any real seed.

It was clear that Job knew the dream and accusations were not his to own, but he does give us a slight insight into Eliphaz's own character in Job 6:27, "Yea, ye overwhelm the fatherless, and ye dig a pit for your friend."

Job had personal knowledge of Eliphaz, and it was clear he had some issues where his own character was concerned. Job recognized that Eliphaz was trying to dig a pit for him, while Job could not discern any hidden iniquity or perverse thing in his life or ways. This is when Job challenged him to be content to look upon him as the man he knew he was, and he would know if he was lying. If Eliphaz could not honestly look upon Job without any personal bias, then he needed to silence any further accusations against his character and return his righteousness.[11]

Since Eliphaz convinced himself that the dream was given to him to warn Job, he became blatant in his next statement in Job 5:1, "Call now, if there be any that will answer thee; and to which of the saints wilt thou turn?" Consider what Eliphaz was saying to Job, "If you are in such straights, call out and see who will answer you and who will you turn to, to stand in the gap." It seemed cruel and mocking because it was clear that Job's ordeal caused him to unfairly lose his standing in his community.

Eliphaz continued to present his case that Job's problem had to do with sin, but he said something that revealed his hypocrisy in Job 5:7, "Yet man is born unto trouble, as the sparks fly upward." Eliphaz has been presenting a case that a righteous man would be immune from experiencing such affliction that had come upon Job, but he admits that man is born unto trouble.

Man came under a terrible curse of suffering and death in the Garden of Eden. Jesus said that we would have much tribulation and throughout the Psalms we can see where King David experienced much persecution, but I guess what Eliphaz was saying is that everyone but Job was born unto trouble. In spite of what Eliphaz was trying to put on righteous Job, the truth is, "many are the afflictions of the righteous."[12] Eliphaz was implying that Job's trouble was not a matter of being in the world and living life but because he was a hypocrite.

Again, I think this speaks of how Job, before his ordeal, indeed had right standing before his friends and community. Eliphaz's contradictory statement reminds me of someone who possibly had high regard for Job, but now Job, due to no fault of his own, had fallen off the pedestal, exposing the frailty of humanity causing

---

[11] Job 6:28,29
[12] Genesis 3:17-19; Psalm 34:19; John 16:33

Eliphaz to fearfully and angrily trip over his own attitudes and theology.

Job actually made reference to this fact in Job 6:18-21. Job pointed out that it is not unusual for people to perceive they are on the right path, only to discover they have turned aside and are heading nowhere. As a comparison, certain troops and companies start out with a clear mission but become confused and what they put their hope in is brought to shame. He goes on to say to Eliphaz, "For now ye are nothing; ye see my casting down, and are afraid."

It was clear to Job that his plight had brought great fear on Eliphaz. After all, if such an ordeal can happen to Job, a righteous man in his generation, it can happen to anyone. Regardless of how righteous one is, he or she will never be immune from the troubles and afflictions of life. In fact, at such times our light is able to shine brighter if we allow our faith to fan the flame of our light.

At this point Eliphaz tells Job what he would do in his place. He would seek God and he would commit his cause. Eliphaz assumed Job had never sought God in his time of distress, but we know he worshipped him after he lost his family and in Job's response in Job 6:8, we know that he had made requests to the Lord. We even see him struggle before the Lord in Job 7:17-21.

In these Scriptures Job admits the obvious, why should God consider and visit mere man in his plight, but he could not help but ask the obvious, "How long will you depart from me and leave me alone, while I swallow down my spittle?" He goes on to plead to the preserver of men by clearly stating that if he has sinned, what shall he do about it? This shows us Job had already sought God about any possible sin, but it appeared there was a mark against him because for some reason his unknown transgression had not been pardoned or his iniquity had not been taken away.

The problem for Job is that the wrestling match was proving to be unbearable and his desire to sleep in the sweetness of death appeared so close, yet so far away, but he also acknowledged that he would not be able to resolve the matter in this life. Only heaven could answer the haunting question of his mind, but perhaps he was like the Apostle Paul who in 2 Corinthians 5:8 and 9 pointed out that whether one is present or absent from the body, one continues to labor so that the servant can be accepted by the Lord.

Consider for a moment if Job had not finished his course, we would not have the book of Job. Clearly, Job left his mark on his generation and while he was struggling with his great ordeal where death seemed so sweet to his tormented soul, he would have found such comfort if he had been allowed to see down the line the great mark his ordeal would leave on generations to follow, but faith rarely allows you to see down the line. Faith is what allows you to walk through the darkness while trusting God to keep your feet on the narrow path so you will not slip into some great abyss.

Job's loss was great, his suffering indescribable, and his struggle an intense fire, but consider what it means for those who have somewhat walked in the same path. The witness he left behind will always prove comforting to those who find no comfort in this world, his example serves as a light of hope in great darkness, and his resolve a point of courage that allows one the means to continue on regardless of the darkness and intense heat of the ovens.

Upon Eliphaz's instruction to Job as to what he should do in Job 5:13-27, he expounded on the great character and unsearchable ways of God. He spoke of His justice, His care towards His people, His deliverance, and His many promises to those who are truly upright before Him.

Clearly Eliphaz was right about God, but wrong about the situation. The one wrong conclusion that nullified everything he said, bringing him close to blasphemy by falsely accrediting something to God, was that God was punishing or chastising Job for some sin.[13] This revealed that Eliphaz was priggish and as a result there was no bend of humility in his character and no real consideration when it came to Job's plight.

It did not matter how much Job tried to explain the debate in his own soul because there was no conviction of sin, Eliphaz would not hear any of it. In his mind, Job stood guilty before God. After all, he had a dream to confirm it as being so.

The Scoffer
(Job 15)

It is important to keep in mind that Bildad and Zophar were in agreement with Eliphaz's conclusion that there had to be some type of hidden sin in Job's life, and he was either being chastised or tasting God's wrath. As we will see in the following chapters, before Eliphaz's second presentation each man had his own approach to the matter and Job would answer each presentation, and remain unmoved by their conclusions. As we will see, in the case of Bildad, he initially approached this debate from a pious premise and used methods to get Job to see that there could be no other explanation for his plight but some hidden sin.

Zophar's initial attempt came at Job from the angle of a type of self-righteous indignation that if Job was the man he professed to be, he would not even allow God's reputation to be questioned as a means to justify himself. In such indignation one will even appeal to God to confirm what the accuser perceives to be the obvious conclusions.

Each man would stand behind God's character in a so-called "defense" of His reputation, but Job was not accusing God of unfairly doing anything. He was questioning, wrestling, and lamenting with the "whys" behind his circumstances, but he was

---

[13] Job 5:17,18

not accusing God of being directly behind them. It is true Job recognized that what befell him could not have happened without God permitting it, but he also knew without a doubt that God's ways, regardless of how man perceives them, are true, right, just, and holy and would stand in the end.

These companions were right about God, but wrong about His part in the plight of Job. It is not enough to know something, if it is not applicable at that time it will pervert what is known and twist what is possible to fit personal conclusions, causing evil fruits of confusion, misunderstanding, and despair to come to rest like a heavy blanket on an innocent party.

Eliphaz started from the premise of a dreamer, certain that his dream was meant for Job. He was convinced if Job was the righteous man he thought himself to be, he would eventually see the light and naturally respond to his presentation of it and his instruction to him in a right way. Granted, Job's halo was tarnished in his eyes, but Job could somewhat redeem himself if only he would accept Eliphaz's interpretation.

Job took issue with Eliphaz's interpretation and misconstrued conclusions. He had most likely silently wrestled before the Lord from the beginning about what was happening to him. His theology did not make sense, his present situation was taunting him, and his search to understand had created greater darkness.

Job was seeking God perspective, and not man's mere interpretation that at best would skip across the bitter stream of indifference to personally avoid the depth of conflict it could cause in his own soul if personally faced with it. With God, Job was met with complete silence, but now that the door was open, he was finding himself the target of loud accusations that revealed misunderstandings, misconstrued attitudes, assumed speculations, and presumed conclusions. Job was not about to leave finite man in his limited capacity with the final word on the matter. After all, it was his plight, his personal wrestling match, and his path he had been walking, and it became obvious there were probably few who could ever understand the depth of his sorrow or his struggle.

Eliphaz's idea that his dream and diplomatic approach would sway his friend came from fanciful notions. He no doubt perceived in his imagination that if Job did not see it his way, he would surely see the reason of the other two companions. After all, their presentations would have seemed brilliant to any wise, thinking man. It was obvious to the three of them the problem rested with Job, and Job needed to rectify it.

This brings us to the digression of man in a debate where the opposition refuses to see it his way. In the mind of his companions, Job was in the minority and should have conceded on that alone. The fact that he seemed to become more unreasonable in each confrontation confirmed the speculation of his companions that there was indeed something amiss in Job's character.

As Christians we know the world's majority is often standing on the wrong side of truth and eternity. We know if a saint is standing with God, they are in the majority because all of heaven is behind them.

No doubt Job felt outnumbered but he did not perceive that he was on the wrong side of eternity. He became bolder in his claims about God, not weaker. His was standing on what he knew was true about God and the relationship he had with Him, and no one could sway him from that truth.

Eliphaz started out a dreamer who was shot down by a harsh dose of reality. Once a dream loses its expectation, it will produce scoffing. We see this scenario in today's world. People had been told for generations Jesus is coming. No doubt there were those who put their hope in the idea of the promise instead of the Promised One and the result is that many are now the scoffers who say, "Where is He?" In fact, I remember talking to such a scoffer after Bible Study. He asked in a scoffing matter, "Where is He?" If I had been prepared, I would have told him, "His coming

126

will be soon and you are proof of that, for in the last days there will be scoffers who say, 'Where is His coming?'"[14]

It is clear that Eliphaz was losing his patience with Job, but he was not about to give up without going some more rounds. After all, he would remain true to his convictions regardless of the past facts that he was aware of concerning Job's conduct and confirmed by him in his own presentation. Now let us consider the path of a dreamer that becomes a scoffer.

The first thing that Eliphaz pointed out in Job 15:2 is how can a wise man utter vain knowledge and fill his belly with the east wind? Eliphaz was questioning Job's wisdom based on the fact that he didn't silently accept his companions' conclusions. He goes on to accuse Job's speech of being unprofitable and incapable of bringing any good to the situation. In a sense he was accusing him of being a blowhard.[15]

He proceeded to tell Job that he had cast off all fear of God and had kept his prayer back from God to avoid the obvious reality of his plight.[16] Scoffers can't help but question the intelligence of those who would believe contrary to their biased conclusions regardless of opposing facts that have been established.

Job would not have any of Eliphaz's disrespect when he set the record straight in Job chapters 16 and 17. He called his companions most miserable comforters. Job turns Eliphaz's accusation about his words back on him. If his words were as vain and lame as Eliphaz claimed they were, why did he even bother to address them? Clearly, Job's words had hit some mark of truth or why did he feel so emboldened to take issue with him to set the record straight?[17]

In Job 17:4, Job declared that God had hid understanding from them. He goes to say that they may speak flattery to their friends

---

[14] 2 Peter 3:2-3
[15] Job 15:3
[16] Job 15:4
[17] Job 16:2-3

but have made him a byword of the people. He pointed out upright men would be astonished at what happened to him and even the innocent would stir themselves up against the hypocrisy that was taking place. He pointed out that a righteous man would hold on to his way and that those with clean hands would come out stronger in their convictions.[18]

Eliphaz was clearly focusing on what Job was saying in order to prove his point instead of discerning Job's actions. Job made mention of this in Job 16:15-22. He had put sackcloth on his skin and wept as he walked through the shadows of death. His prayer was pure and he knew that what had befallen him was not due to any injustice on his part, and even though his friends scorned him, he still cried out to God. If only he had an intercessor to stand in the gap, to plead for him when the opportunity afforded itself. He lamented that times for intercession will pass once one passes from this world.

The one who is losing the debate will change the subject. To Eliphaz, Job's problem was no longer a hidden sin, but an obvious sin and it all came down to the fact that Job was not about to accept his three companions' conclusion to his plight. At this point Eliphaz is exalting himself as the one with authority whose mind can't be changed because Job is the one who condemned himself.[19]

Scoffers not only think your stand shows you to be foolish, but they will exalt themselves in a place of authority to put you in your proper place. In their mind, you have lost your right to possess any platform.

It is important to note how Eliphaz asked Job certain questions. He asked him if he was the first man born or whether he was made before the hills. He goes on to question him as to whether he had heard the secret of God and does he now hold such wisdom for himself? Are the consolations of God small to Job? Eliphaz

---

[18] Job 17:4-9
[19] Job 15:6

queried about what does Job know that they don't know and who among them are older than his father, for their fathers did not hide such wisdom from them. These questions were to knock Job down from what was considered his self-righteous platform.[20]

At this point Eliphaz asked him if his heart carried him away from truth and what has he been turning a blind eye to when it came to his own character. When did his spirit turn against God, allowing such words to fly out of his mouth? How is it that a man born of woman can perceive himself to be clean and righteous?[21]

These are good questions, but Eliphaz was asking the wrong man. Job never made the claims that Eliphaz was putting upon him. The fact that Job was not agreeing with his companions' conclusions and was answering their claims had nothing to do with accusing God or justifying himself. Eliphaz again could not get past the mindset that for God to be and remain righteous in his mind when it came to Job, Job had to be guilty of iniquity.

It is at this point that Eliphaz hides behind God's character. He declares the untrustworthiness of man for God does not put complete trust in His saints for the heavens are not clean before Him. If the heavens are not even clean before Him, how much more are the abominable acts and filth of man who drink from the waters of iniquity?[22]

Eliphaz instructs Job to hear him and what he has seen, he will declare. To Eliphaz, these matters must be so because they were told by their fathers who received it and did not hide it.[23] A scoffer wants you to agree with their logic or wisdom. It is obvious to them; therefore, it should be obvious to you, and all the person needs to do is see it based on what has been established.

Indifferent opinions rarely apply to the plight of man, limited knowledge may be applied but only if it results in wisdom being

---

[20] Job 15:7-10
[21] Job 15:12-14
[22] Job 15:15,16
[23] Job 15:17,18

established as a witness that something is so. Wisdom is applicable when truth and discretion reveal heavenly inspiration that is able to truly identify with and enter in with a person.

There are different wisdoms. There is worldly wisdom and it is called "common sense." Common sense is usually the combination of experience and what is practical. There is a fleshly wisdom and it is called "intelligence." This wisdom is accredited to intelligence in light of its ability of deduction. There is carnal wisdom that can be clever, but is always self-serving and treacherous.

It is true that our fathers do pass down certain veins of wisdom that come from the world and deduction. This wisdom can be practical in matters of life, functionable in the activities of life, and beneficial in the demands of life, but the wisdom from heaven is inspirational, discreet, realistic, practical, and always beneficial whether it comes to instruction or application. James clearly speaks about this wisdom in James 3:17.

It is clear that Eliphaz's idea of wisdom was not inspirational because it was not from God. It was a matter of his own deduction and at first it appeared clever and gentle, but when tested with opposition, it became scoffing.

In Job 17:10, Job makes it clear that there is not one wise man among his companions. They have basically called his goodness evil, and the evil falling on him as being just and good. They have robbed him of purpose, defiled the deep thoughts of his heart, changed his night into a false light of hope, and shortened the light of truth by their darkness. If he silently waited before them, they would bury all hope, and because of them he had to make his bed of defense in darkness that promised no light of truth and unity when it came to reasoning with them.[24]

To confirm his personal conclusions about Job, Eliphaz spoke of the plight of the wicked. It is the wicked man that travails with pain all of his days and the number of his days are hidden from

---

[24] Job 17:11-13; Isaiah 5:20

him. His prosperity shall be destroyed, and he sees no way out of the darkness and waits for death to come upon him. He wanders in his trouble and anguish as fear grips his soul, for he knows he has stretched his hand out against God and has opposed Him. He heaps up for himself the things of the world as he dwells in desolate cities and in uninhabited houses, but in the end, he will find himself poor because his ways are that of vanity and he will find himself in the congregation of the hypocrites because he has conceived mischief according to the ways of deceit.[25]

In Job 16, it becomes obvious that since Job's companions chose to ignore his plight, he goes on to explain the psychology of pain. After all, it not only plagues the physical body but if there is no support, it greatly assaults the mental and emotional aspects of a person. In Job 16:6, Job begins to talk about the grief it caused and he goes on to speak of how it has digressed into a mental weariness due to their accusations, causing wrinkles because of the emotional despair that constantly besieges him due to the wrath they have leveled against him. He sees them as trying to whittle him down with their sharp words as they strike against his resolve, making it appear that God has delivered him into the hands of the wicked. He explained how his eye is dim by reason of sorrow and all of his members are as shadows.[26]

Before they affronted him, his soul was at ease in his suffering, but their accusations had broken him down and their attacks made him feel as if he had been taken by the neck by a cruel animal that was trying to shake him to pieces while setting him up to be utterly destroyed. They constantly shot allegations at him while trying to pull him down into a pit of bitterness so every area of resistance could be brought to ruin.[27]

Eliphaz could not identify Job's real moral deviation in his previous discourse, but Job's unwillingness to accept the

---

[25] Job 15:20-35
[26] Job 16:7-11; 17:7
[27] Job 16:11-14

presentations of these three men supposedly revealed in Eliphaz's mind the real area of Job's guilt. It rested with his words. It is true that words expose the heart attitude, but Eliphaz's contention had nothing to do with any real sin; rather, it was based on the fact that Job would not concede to their presentations of his so-called "guilt." Eliphaz accused Job of uttering iniquity which he felt revealed to him that his tongue was crafty and as a result his mouth was condemning him and his lips testified against him.[28]

It is easy enough to see why Job was in complete distress over his companions' onslaught of accusations. However, Job maintained his faith and confidence that one day the truth would come out about his plight. His faith took center stage when he declared, "Also now, behold, my witness is in heaven, and my record is on high" (Job 16:19).

Job knew the truth and would not accept his companions' claims. He knew in the end that the witness of heaven would verify what he knew was true and that the record in heaven would confirm his witness as being so. This clearly showed that Job knew who would ultimately settle the matter, the righteous Judge of heaven.

Rigid Moralist
(Job 22)

In Eliphaz's final presentation, you see a scoffer becoming a mighty moralist who resorts to the worse type of severity as to his accusations that were based on rigid, religious standards. No matter what approach a dreamer like Eliphaz takes, he will eventually become a scoffer towards reality, ultimately ending up becoming more rigid and severe in his judgments against anyone who disagrees.

---

[28] Matthew 15:16-20

Keep in mind, each attack leveled at Job by his three companions escalated with bolder indictments being directed at him. Bildad in his presentation implied that no dignity should be allotted to Job in Job 18 because he would not accept the obvious conclusion, while Zophar in Job 20 showed nothing but disdain for Job in his speech. When you start to put all the incredible accusations together that were flung at Job, you have to shake your head as you realize most people would have become silent as they slithered in some corner to lick their battered body, their shredded mental state, and their frayed emotions.

Eliphaz asked a simple question, "Can a man be profitable unto God, as he that is wise may be profitable unto himself?"[29] Oswald Chambers in his book, *Baffled to Fight Better,* talked about how the religious phases people go through never really touches the reality of a matter. Chambers pointed out that a person's insistence on certain sound doctrine ends up becoming chaff with no real substance or authority behind it. He goes on to say, "Every denominationalist is certain that the crowd who does not agree with what "we" call our sound principles must be wrong; he never imagines that the 'Job' type of man can be right with God."[30]

Eliphaz clearly fit in this category. He goes on to set up his case against Job. Scripture shows us God takes pleasure in the righteous, but Eliphaz was implying that God could not take pleasure in his former friend's righteousness because he was simply making his ways right in his own eyes, convincing himself God was in agreement.[31]

He goes on to inquire of Job, would not the Lord reprove him out of fear for his soul and why would Job not enter into agreement with God's judgment. He goes on to confirm his case by accusing

[29] Job 22:2
[30] pg. 96
[31] Job 22:3

Job of having great wickedness and infinite iniquities. Again, I must point out that Job was not accused of being a transgressor.[32]

A transgressor is a lawbreaker and the terms used against Job reveal that the Law of Moses had not yet been given to the children of Israel at Mount Sinai. The Apostle Paul clearly pointed out the Law of Moses was given to show us we are all transgressors of His Law, making us sinners.[33] As we will see, even without the Law of Moses, these men understood what constituted righteousness before God. Whatever was established as laws came from their fathers and once again it may have been laws that Noah passed down to his descendants, but we also know the law of God was written on the conscience of man.[34]

We know in the beginning of this debate that Eliphaz acknowledged Job's righteousness, but in his desperation, he accused him of being a different person altogether. Apparently, contrary to his former life and actions, Job either was a great actor by portraying righteousness or he was a deluded hypocrite, because Eliphaz blatantly accused him of taking away from his brother and the poor, as well as afflicting the widows and fatherless as they cried to the Lord, causing His wrath to wax hot against him. Supposedly, Job perverted his judgment towards others, oppressed the vulnerable, kept water back from the thirsty and bread from the hungry, as well as removed landmarks and robbed the fatherless. According to Eliphaz, Job's wicked deeds became snares around him and fear of its consequences were now troubling him.[35]

Eliphaz's unwarranted and unproven accusations were slanderous. He actually gave himself away when he implied all

---

[32] Job 22:4,5

[33] Romans 3:19,20

[34] Compare Job 22:6-9 with Exodus 22:22-24; Deuteronomy 24:17; Proverbs 23:10-11; and James 1:27. Also see Romans 1:20.

[35] Job 4:3,4; 22:6-10

that Job had done was in darkness, while rightfully pointing out nothing can be hidden from God because He is in heaven and beholds the stars and judges through dark clouds. He also was accusing Job of saying that God couldn't see him even though He walks the circuit of heaven.[36]

Clearly Eliphaz was assuming something he had not personally witnessed. Slander has no intention of seeking the truth or justice in a matter because it springs from prideful presumption, where the will of man makes his conclusion as being truth, regardless of what is so.[37] It is a type of self-delusion that is beyond reason but if it has a religious connotation to it; therefore, it is deemed as being what must be so. Since it lines up to the accepted theology of God, it should also make sense to any normal thinking person.

Job's response to the slander was realistic. He knew that in the courtroom of his companions' minds he stood guilty of something that was not so. He could defend himself which he did, but he knew they perceived him as being guilty and they had to make sure he remained so.

Job knew there was only one who could at that point plead his cause and that was God. He knew that he could actually present his case before Him, knowing how the righteous judge would respond. This again reveals Job's faith towards the character of God.[38] It was clear that he knew God and understood His great justice.

The great patriarch goes on to say that he was confident the Lord would not plead against him with His great power; rather, he would put strength in him to stand in confidence of proclaiming a righteous verdict. Job goes on to say that it was at the place of God's righteousness that the righteous could dispute with Him,

---

[36] Job 22:11-14
[37] 2 Peter 2:10
[38] Job 23:3-5

knowing that He would ultimately deliver them. The problem that Job was having is not with the righteous character of God, but with the fact that for some reason He had remained hidden from him and silent in, and during, his plight.[39]

Eliphaz asked Job if he had marked the way that the wicked had previously trodden and how they were cut down out of time by a flood. This is in reference to the flood of Noah. According to Eliphaz these wretched people told the Lord to depart from them because they saw no need for Him to be in their midst in spite of the fact that He was the one who filled their houses with good things. In the end, the righteous will see God's judgment on such people and the innocent will end up mocking and scorning them.[40]

As a result, in Job 24:1, we see Job acknowledging that nothing can be hidden from God, and that He has their days numbered and seasons set for judgment, but he goes on to state what he understood about what constituted righteous acts before their holy God in Job 24. He challenged his companions in Job 24:25 to prove he was a liar and his speech worthless if what he stated was not so.

Job also recognized that even if a person knows God, it does not stop them from walking in the ways of unrighteousness. They still can remove landmarks, and violently take away the flocks and feed whosoever they will. He even acknowledged that such individuals rebel against the light because they do not know the ways of righteousness or abide in its path.[41]

Job laid out the sins and case against such individuals in Job 24:3-18 and admitted that even though it appears that God does not regard the wrong done to those who groan under these wicked people's grave oppression, there will be an end to their ways. He made some statements as to their end in Job 24:17-23, that death

---

[39] Job 23:6-9
[40] Job 22:15-19
[41] Job 24:2,3, 13

will shadow and torment them, while their portion in this world will be cursed and the grave will consume them. Such individuals shall be forgotten and the worm shall feed on them, which is associated to the work of the grave and hell.[42] Their wickedness will be as a broken tree and everything they touch will prove barren and useless to others, and even though opportunities are allotted them along the way, they will pass them by as they use their power to draw others. In the end, they can't be sure of preserving or keeping their own life, and even though these wicked people may encounter some security in this world, God eyes are always upon their ways.

Job concluded with this statement in Job 24:24, "They are exalted for a little while, but are gone and brought low; they are taken out of the way as all *other*, and cut off as the tops of the ears of corn."

As we study what Job stated, we can see that it became clearer to him that sometimes God does remain silent for a season. His faith took on a greater pose of assurance and we can see this very fact in Job 23:10-17. Job has been in a wrestling match of the "whys" behind his plight, but in this set of Scriptures, it is becoming obvious that he landed on the runway of peace in order to come to a place of abiding rest.

It is here that he acknowledged his ordeal was not about some moral deviation in his character or some sin he had unknowingly committed, but that it was about the testing of his faith. In Job 23:10, he made this statement, "But he knoweth the way that I take: *when* he hath tried me, I shall come forth as gold."

Job knew that God knew that his way had been considered righteous and that after the testing of his faith, he would come forth as gold, pure before God, prized by Him, and ultimately used by Him. Job had confidence because of his walk before the Lord. His

---

[42] Job 19:26; 21:26; Isaiah 66:24; Mark 9:44, 48

137

feet had not slipped from the path, nor had he ever gone back from keeping the Lord's commandments. He valued His words more necessary than food. He pointed out how God is immutable in his ways, powerful in His doings and willing and able to perform what He had appointed for his life.[43]

It was true Job was troubled at His presence and had trepidation towards what it all meant, but he recognized that it was God who held and maintained his tender heart towards Him as He allowed trouble and dismay to be his companions. His conclusion was as one established by faith, that since he was not cut off and kept from facing this great time of trouble, God still must have a plan for him.[44]

Bob Sorge stated that God reserves the greatest victories for the vessels that have known the greatest brokenness. It has also been said by Doctor Forsythe, "There is no reality without struggling. If you are not called to wrestle, it is only because the wrestling is being done for you."

Job admitted at one point he was but a mere clay vessel in Job 10:9, but at this point he was recognizing that the trial of his faith had made him into a gold vessel, fit for the master's use. Job would have certainly related to what the Apostle Paul said about the different vessels in 2 Timothy 2:20-21,

> But in a great house there are not only vessels of gold and of silver, but also of wood and of earth; and some to honour, and some to dishonour. If a man therefore purge himself from these, he shall be a vessel unto honour, sanctified, and meet for the master's use, *and* prepared unto every good work.

---

[43] Job 23:11-14
[44] Job 22:15-17

10

The Pious Philosopher
(Job 8)

*If we want to grow in faith we must be open to
listening to our own stories, perhaps familiar
or forgotten, where we have not mined the rich
deposit of God's presence. With better eyes
and ears we will sense how God has worked to
redeem even our most tragic experiences.*
(Dan Allender)

The next man we come to in this great debate is Bildad. His initial approach to Job was to ask Job questions. Questions are used for various reasons, but they have a strategical base to them. Some ask questions to cause one to consider what is being said in order to ponder or meditate before answering. This approach is to open the individual up to have a constructive dialogue with the inquirer, others ask questions because they do not know the information needed to proceed or have failed to listen in the first place and missed it, and there are those who ask questions to set someone up to fall into a trap.

The Pharisees in the New Testament are a good example of the latter tactic. They used this strategy many times with Jesus and He often responded with another question. The Pharisees were trying to cleverly set Jesus up with their mode of examination, but Jesus asked questions to challenge the religious leaders in such a way as to cause them to stop, listen, mediate, and then answer their own question. It is from this basis that Jesus shared insights, and sometimes parables. For Bildad, he would use suppositions, and as we will see, Job used them as well.

Consider Bildad's first question in Job 8:2. It is important because it gives insight into his attitude about Job. Keep in mind, Eliphaz had presented his first case in light of a dream, but Job would not accept his presentation and now the next line of prosecution rested with Bildad.

Bildad asked Job how long he will speak about such things because all he was doing was spewing out hot air. It was clear that Bildad was not interested in Job's answer because he already stipulated that it would be nothing more than hot air, an exaggeration.

When you read Job 8:3, it was logically clear to Bildad that Job was under judgment. After all, God does not pervert judgment or justice. It is easy when a matter does not personally affect you to emotionally divorce yourself from it as a means to downplay it and make it irrelevant to what you consider the real crux of the matter. At such times it is easy for a person to become a philosopher as to what they perceive to be true about life while ignoring what is true. At such times a person with enough theology can prove to be quite pious in expounding on what is morally true and right regardless of what is obvious.

In the minds of Job's companions, there was no way God would pour judgment on a righteous man, because God's will for the righteous man is that of blessings and promises. It is true God will not pour judgment on a righteous man; however, they failed to realize that He will allow the righteous to be tested with adversity.

Satan was behind Job's plight and God had permitted Satan to come against Job while still holding the reins with His sovereignty, knowing the character of Job's faith. It was in His providential will that God allowed certain things to happen to Job in order to bring forth a greater testimony that remains today for us to examine and consider.

In their "noble" attempt to protect what Job's companions perceived was God's righteous reputation, they had to slander Job of his upright reputation. In their minds, the visible circumstances warrant their conclusion about Job that one had to be unrighteous in their character to experience such circumstances. These men used assumptions to put Job on trial while standing on presumptions to condemn him with false accusations and slanders.

In Job 8:4 Bildad begins with the word, "if." This word sets one up to consider the validity to a matter, and is not a word to be used in the arena of option. When Jesus used it in the call to discipleship, the word, "if" was establishing a prerequisite as to what it would mean to follow Him, but in this case Bildad was using it to show that Job's plight was not what he was portraying it to be.[1]

If you can't convince the person that their plight is due to character, then you must downplay the intensity of the person's plight. After all, a man only reaps what he sows; therefore, Job is reaping what he is sowing or he is exaggerating the effect it has and was having on his life.[2]

Consider what Bildad was implying in Job 8:4, that Job's children's fate was a matter of their sin being judged, and then he goes on to say in Job 8:5, "If thou wouldest seek unto God betimes, and make thy supplication to the Almighty." Here is the supposition that if Job had stood in the gap for his children and himself, he would not be in his present situation. Keep in mind, we were told that Job served as a mediator for his children in case they had sinned.[3] However, Bildad was putting all the responsibility and blame of these terrible losses on Job, while trying to maintain that what befell Job's children was just.

[1] Matthew 16:24-26
[2] Galatians 6:7,8
[3] Job 1:5

Bildad's attitude points to what is considered the gospel of temperament. His logic is that all Job had to do was change his temperament towards a matter regardless of the facts and it would change how he looked at it. Those who adhere to this type of gospel refuse to change their creeds in spite of the circumstances, revealing their indifference to the reality of a matter.

In Job's response to Bildad in Job 9:2 and 3, he pointed out if the just God chose to be against him, where would he be at the present? Clearly, if Job was under great judgment as his companions implied, he would most likely be dead. Job also acknowledged that if he did contend with God, he could not get Him to answer no matter what he did. Even prayer and intercession can't influence God from His sovereign position and His plan unless He wills it or allows it to be so.[4]

Even though this may sound cynical on Job's part, it implies he is coming to the end of his theology, and once a person does, his or her faith can be activated that will allow the struggling soul to land on the runway of assurance and rest. God does not have to explain Himself to man. Man is the clay and God the Potter, and it is in the ovens that the potter's touch and involvement with the clay vessels completely ceases. It is at this point the vessel must rest in the potter's ability to bring forth a vessel fit for His use and glory by putting the vessel in the right position in the fiery oven to bring out the vessel's potential. Meanwhile, the vessel must not become focused on or overwhelmed by the process.[5]

When God becomes quiet it is usually to bring man to the end of his understanding about what he thinks he knows about all matters pertaining to Him and His will and way. It is at such a point that man must either choose to go into unbelief or to trust the Lord

---

[4] Job 9:11-14
[5] Romans 9:20-23; 2 Timothy 2:19-21

that He is the I AM, ever present in all matters, in control over all events, and totally aware.

This is the critical point of faith. It is a type of crossroad that can cause man to rest on who God is even though the stormy emotional and mental deluge is still raging in his soul. He may have to wrestle with resentment, put down anger, and climb over despair, but resolve and peace can finally come to his soul once he puts all of his worries, struggles, and concerns on the Lord. It is at such a time that the saint will realize it is okay to say, "I don't know, but it does not matter because God is *GOD*, Eloah, the One who has it all under control and knows how to bring about His perfect will."

Some of the greatest modern-day criticisms of Job comes from those who think they can influence God, control Him, and change the outcome of a matter with their words. Whether it is with confession, declarations, or using God's Words and promises against Him to claim some right or point of victory, they perceive their words hold much more power than Eloah's sovereign will in a matter. They present God as being someone who can be emotionally moved, flattered, conned, or told how to interpret His Word and His promises in order to maintain His position in their minds, regardless of His timing or whether it meets His righteous criteria. Such a scenario puts God to a foolish test, while setting up the deluded individual for a great fall that will land them in the depths of unbelief and despair. These types of teachings are heretical and set people up to teeter on the abyss of insanity because their reality is so fragile.

Job understood the score and he knew that Bildad was proving to be a windbag, but it appears from his statement in Job 9:3, he also was beginning to realize that there were big gaps in his theology. He had come to the end of his theological understanding and recognized he could not explain what seemed to be obvious to the physical eye, while maintaining sound judgments according to intellectual deduction based on accepted theology.

It is at this point of such concession from the righteous of "not knowing a matter," "of the ineptness to understand it", or "the inability to make any real scriptural or religious sense out of it," that people like Job can come across as hypocrites, or as one losing faith, or being exposed as an agnostic.

The mysterious ways of God will bring the best of us to places of great perplexity, and in our struggle to understand or make sense out of that which has been hidden from us, we will appear to be agnostic. A committed agnostic knows there is more they can know and as a result seeks enlightenment, but it is always outside of the Holy Spirit. However, when a saint comes up against such mystery, he or she knows only the Holy Spirit can bring such enlightenment, and that each revelation will not be brought to each of us as we think we need it, or as we flounder in desperation to know it, or in light of false accusations.[6] It will come when God so wills it and not before. It is for this reason that Oswald Chambers states in his book, *Baffled to Fight Better*, "A Christian is an avowed agnostic intellectually; his attitude is, 'I have reached the limit of my knowledge, and I humbly accept the revelation of God given by Jesus Christ.'"[7]

In my experience the light of revelation never comes until God has accomplished what He has set out to do in the believer. In the life of the saint, the light breaking through the darkness is never quick enough when they feel they are teetering on the edge of the great abyss where complete destruction awaits, but when the light does come, it brings great comfort and joy.

In Job 8:5 and 6, Bildad presents two other suppositions. If Job would seek the Lord and make his supplications to the Almighty.

---

[6] Ephesians 1:17,18; Hebrews 6:4-6
[7] pg. 54

If he was truly pure and upright the Lord would no longer be indifferent towards his plight; rather, He would make Job's habitation of righteousness prosperous.

Again, Job is being accused as being prayerless and defiled. He is told that he could awaken the Lord in supplication and He would make his righteousness to once again prosper. Here is a hint that Bildad recognized that Job was known as a righteous man before his plight.

Job once again took issue with Bildad's deduction. Job made reference to how God is wise in heart and mighty in strength and a righteous person would never harden himself against God and really expect to prosper.[8] Even though he was struggling in his own soul, Job knew the score when it came to God and true righteousness. Job's struggle was not a matter of rebellion, and as one who had been counted righteous by God, he knew God was still wise in His judgments and strong in His ways, and that no righteous person would harden himself against God and not expect judgment.

It is from this point that Job expounds on who God is. As I read his discourse in Job 9:5-10, I can see no point of accusation coming from Job towards the character of God and no malice because of his plight; rather, I see him declaring that God does great and wondrous things that can't be counted. These are the declarations of a man who has kept God in His rightful place in spite of the great inner struggle going on in his soul and the debacle surrounding him.

In Job 8:7, Bildad approached Job with a platitude. A platitude is a banal, a trite or stale remark. When a person uses a platitude, it is to make him or herself appear wise in their ignorance. Platitudes reveal either a state of ignorance or emotional indifference because the person using them has come to the end

---

[8] Job 9:4

145

of his or her case, and has no idea where to go. In a sense, they have hit an empty place and must scramble to fill it with something that sounds somewhat engaging and intelligent.

Platitudes clearly point to one operating from the gospel of temperament. This is where the accuser or instructor remains emotionally indifferent while trying to influence the mood of the other individual by stirring up a bit of sentiment or passion by pointing to some point of wisdom or a promise.

The platitude was, "Though thy beginning was small, yet thy latter end should greatly increase." This platitude is basic in that we all start small and if we have integrity of righteousness the latter will prove to be greater. There is a principle attached to it. We are not to despise the days of small beginnings and once God steps on the scene, the latter will always prove to be greater than the former.[9]

Job admitted that the Lord could go by him and he would not see him and pass on and not discern it. However, faith does not rest on what it sees, but what it knows based on what is of spirit and truth.[10] Jesus even brought this point out to Thomas in John 20:29, "Thomas, because thou hast seen me, thou hast believed: blessed *are* they that have not seen, and *yet* have believed."

It was pointed out by Job that once a matter was settled in heaven, who could hinder Eloah, while daring to cross examine Him about the wisdom behind the ways He has taken?[11] Job struggled with, not what God does, but where He was in his plight. Nothing made sense to Job because what was happening to him was not the way God handles matters.

Job recognized God's sovereignty to do as He wills, but his circumstances were definitely not a matter of God judging him for some grievous sin. There had to be more going on in the spiritual

---

[9] Haggai 2:9; Zechariah 4:10
[10] Job 9:11
[11] Job 9:12

realm that remained hidden from him and until it was revealed, he had to stand on what he knew to be true about God. It is at this point that genuine faith will land and discover inspiration, which will cause someone like Job to have a resurgence take place in his soul that will not only help him to stand up, but for the expectation of real hope to take flight beyond the obvious.

Job understood that no one could withstand God's anger, and there would be no basis of reasoning with Him, but he once again maintained that he did not know what was going on, but nevertheless, he would make supplication to his judge.[12]

In Job 9:16, Job begins with a series of suppositions. Here comes the word "if" from Job. Bildad's suppositions were presented in the light of Job responding the right way in order to make peace with God, but for Job he came from the premise of what appears to be a certain way to the naked eye in light of what was so. It was true that due to God's sovereignty, Job felt his life had been broken by the hand of God, wounded in spite of his innocence, making his life a bitter pill to swallow. But, as we will see, Job brings a contrast in order to highlight his responses to the accusations being cast at him.

The first "if" in Job 9:16 had to do with God hearing Job and answering. Job understood if you seek God in sincerity about a matter, He will answer. This is especially true if sin is present and one is unaware of it, and like David ask the Lord to turn on the searchlight and see if there is any wicked way in him.[13] However, if He didn't answer He still remained who HE IS, a just Judge of all.

Job was in a way admitting it appeared as if God was judging him in Job 9:17 and 18 and if He did, He would still be just in it, but God also knows how to remake a marred vessel. He knew it

---

[12] Job 9:14,15
[13] Psalm 139:23,24

was God who maintained his spiritual and physical life and sent forth all judgment. Job goes on with his suppositions. "If I tried to justify myself in some way, my own mouth would condemn me, and if I declared I was perfect, I would prove to be perverse. And, if I was perfect, I would still know the plight of my soul and continue to despise the ineptness of my present life." In his conclusion in Job 9:22, God had every right to destroy the perfect and the wicked.

Here Job is admitting he is small before God and in his inept humanity deserving of judgment, but he contrasts this understanding with the ways of the wicked in Job 9:23 and 24. The wicked laugh at the trials of the innocent and the earth is given to hands of the wicked by judges who can be bribed.

Amazingly, Bildad instructs Job in Job 8:8-10 to enquire of the former age by preparing himself to search the wisdom of their fathers. In Bildad's mind he must have concluded that the former age and their fathers would verify what he said to be true. Eliphaz had told Job he would seek God if he was in his shoes, but Bildad tells him to seek the wisdom of their fathers. Perhaps his reasoning was that their lives were short and since God was silent on this matter that their fathers who lived longer, would indeed teach and tell him about such matters according to their heart.

Bildad speaks of the shortness of man's life in Job 8:9-12. Job's response as to the shortness of life was more of a lament that it appeared he might not come to a place of peace. It was clear that his days were fleeing away and instead of seeing the goodness of God triumph, that it was as if his life was being taken as prey, and in a sense, he was being preyed upon by his companions.

Job once again began with suppositions about his plight. He was clearly starting from the bottom and looking through the great darkness of accusations to bring some type of resolution. Obviously, if he didn't have to be realistic about his complaint, he could cast off the heaviness and comfort himself, but he was afraid of his sorrow because he knew Bildad would not hold him innocent. Even if he could wash himself in cold snow and make his hands ever so clean, Bildad would not let him off the hook.[14]

Job's conclusion was based on Bildad's implication that he was a hypocrite whose very hope would be cut off like a spider web. He goes on to imply Job's house would fall, his fruits would die on the vine because his roots are wrapped around nothing more than a heap, and that if God destroys him, Job would not admit his destruction is from His hand.[15]

Job asked a question in Job 9:29, "If I be wicked, why then labour I in vain?" Job did what he did because he had active faith towards God. He knew his commitment and life before the Lord, and if he was such a hypocrite, why did he go to such lengths to ensure that he had right standing and acceptable conduct before the Lord? Job understood that one can only wear the mask of righteousness for a short time before it falls off and the robe of self-righteousness for certain events without others realizing it is a façade. Righteousness has to become a natural inclination in the inner man before it can become a natural, genuine practice in everyday living.

In Job 9:32, Job made it clear that God is not a man as he is and that He is not obligated in any way to answer him, but the struggling patriarch seemed to understand where he could meet the Lord and that was in light of His righteous judgments. That is the one place all righteous people can come into agreement with God.

Bildad's indictment against Job was not over with. It was almost a curse when he stated that the joy of the hypocrite will be

---

[14] Job 9:25-28
[15] Job 8:13-18

short lived and that others will take his place and grow where he stood.[16]

Bildad adds a type of "but," to bring home his point in Job 8:20, "Behold, God will not cast away a perfect *man*, neither will he help the evil doers." He goes on to say God would fill the perfect man's mouth with laughing and his lips with rejoicing, while the wicked would be clothed with much shame and will cease to exist.

Job acknowledged that there was no intercessor or daysman between God and him that could close the gap created by the darkness of the events, and even if God took the rod of adversity away from him and he ceased to be terrified, he still would not unwisely use such liberty to speak of Him from any point of ignorance.[17]

It is important to point out the use of the word, "daysman." A daysman is a type of intercessor who would stand in the position of a priest between God and others. Keep in mind, the Levitical Priesthood was not yet established, and clearly Job served as a daysman for his family, but there was no daysman who would stand on behalf of Job. The truth is one of his companions could have become the daysman, but instead they all became a judge.

Even without a daysman to stand in the gap, when a righteous man comes to the end of his sorrow with no explanation, he must make a choice. Will he become more consumed by his sorrow or will he accept the way something is in order to rest in what he does understand about the character God? This is the real test of a person's faith.

However, Job gives us insight into what he did understand about God when he asked why would God in His infinite knowledge have to inquire after Job's iniquity or search for sin to bring any accusation against him. Job goes on to state that he

---

[16] Job 8:13,14
[17] Job 9:33

knew the Lord knows he is not wicked and that no one could deliver him out of His hand even if he was guilty. There is nothing hidden from God, and if Job was in sin, God's light would automatically expose it and bring conviction.[18] Once again Job had not experienced any such conviction. The Lord's silence left him in a quandary, but he still stood on what he knew to be true.

These companions perceived themselves to be noble by defending God's reputation, but in reality, they were protecting their creeds and every place their creeds were exalted over the truth, God was falsely being credited with activities He was not behind. In order to accomplish this, these men had to turn a blind eye to the real fruits and testimony of Job's life.

Job admitted he was weary with his life and that he had reason to complain and openly speak of the bitterness taking hold in his soul. If he was guilty, he would ask God to not condemn him. He would also ask why He should not contend with him.[19] This may seem presumptuous on Job's part but the truth is he was facing the reality of his plight in light of what He knew about God's desire to forgive and restore the saint.

Job examined his plight while remembering the character and ways of God. He stated that it would not be good for the Lord to oppress him and despise the work of his life while highlighting the counsel of the wicked.[20] Keep in mind, Job deemed the counsel of his companions as being meanspirited, which would put them in the category of wickedness.

He admitted that mere man is limited in what he can see and know and acknowledged that God has no beginning; therefore, He is not subject to time and death.[21] It is from this premise In Job 10:8-11, Job showed he understood the makeup of man. He

---

[18] Job 10:6,7
[19] Job 10:1,2
[20] Job 10:3
[21] Job 10:4,5

started from a simple premise that God fashioned him so why would He destroy him? He had cried out to God to remember that he is but clay, and why would He simply allow him to bring his life to nothing but dust?

This reasoning may seem a bit unnecessary, but for the righteous man who is wading through what is insane, he must often go back to the basics to not only remind himself that life is not for naught because it is marked by eternity. Job goes on to say that God constructed his life, not to simply tear it down on some whim, and it is from this premise that his reasoning lands him on a very simple fact in Job 10:12 and 13, "Thou hast granted me life and favour, and thy visitation hath preserved my spirit. And these *things* hast thou hid in thine heart: I know that this *is* with thee."

Consider what Job is saying. His life had come from God and He had shown him grace and preserved his spirit; and, how did he know these precious truths? Because they were hidden in his heart. Job's faith was clinging to the heavenly gems that were planted in the soil of his heart by God. He would not let go of them

It is from this premise that he put forth more suppositions. If he had sin, he would expect God to mark him and not acquit him from his iniquity. If he was wicked, woe to him and if he is righteous, he still would not lift up his head in accusation or defiance against God. However, regardless of what he knew and understood, he still did not take away his confusion. At this point he asked that the Lord see his afflictions.[22]

Job comes to an important conclusion: Even if God was behind his distress, He was still marvelous. It would not matter if his Maker brought greater witness against him to establish his guilt, He is still the one who brought him out of the womb, and in

---

[22] Job 10:14,15

life, death, or distress, He will always prove to be the source of refuge.[23]

The truth of the matter is the end of man is the grave. His days are few and once he enters it, he will not be heard from again. The dust will cover all of his footprints, the inheritance he leaves will be used up by the generation following, and his legacy wiped out by succeeding generations that have no personal knowledge of him. This is the way of man's life, a clay vessel often formed by adversity, established in the ovens, used to the fullest extent, and then eventually broken to be covered by the sands of time.

The Threat
(Job 18)

When you consider what was leveled at Job, you have to honestly ask yourself, if you have the type of faith that will stand when beaten down, withstand when falsely accused, and endure with sustaining patience through all kinds of abuses? Job is a good example of what it means to possess one's soul in patience.[24]

To possess your soul in patience does not mean you become a doormat and hope to get by, while remaining quiet to avoid confrontation. Nor do you have to accept the conclusion of those around you because they outnumber you, or resort to worldly diplomacy, fake nobility, and/or whimpering because you are being misunderstood, unfairly judged, and falsely accused.

At this point Job had gone a couple of rounds with Eliphaz, and one round a piece with both Bildad and Zophar. He could see that in the debate, any real diplomacy, attempts to reason, or presenting some outward façade of real caring on their part were all gone. The debate was becoming brutal in different ways.

---

[23] Job 10:16-22
[24] Luke 21:19

Eliphaz had started from what seemed like a caring premise only for him to become obnoxious, conceited, and pigheaded. Possibly compelled by Eliphaz's unsuccessful presentation, Bildad started off with more of a frontal attack in his presentation. His mind had already been made up, and it allowed him to serve as the judge and jury towards Job's plight. He became hardheaded in his religious piousness in defending God's "reputation" and indifferent to any part of Job's presentation.

In this second confrontation between Job and Bildad, Bildad is holding to the same approach. He starts out asking a question in Job 18:2. He asked him how long will he speak meaningless words? He stated Job needed to first understand what the real argument was about and then they could have a meaningful discussion.

Think about what Bildad was saying to Job. Until he sees it Bildad's way and comes to the same conclusion as he, there would be no further discussion. He was implying that Job's presentation was non-essential, had no merit to it, and deserved no consideration. Job was being accused by Bildad as being unreasonable, when in reality Bildad was walking around with a board in his eye.[25] He was not only unreasonable but he was making himself unapproachable. He was willing to withdraw any platform from which Job could present his case. In a way he was trying to strip Job of his dignity by implying as before that Job's feelings, struggles, and present plight were greatly exaggerated, or bogus.

What Bildad was implying was cruel and tyrannical. At this point Bildad was coming across as a bully whose threats were meant to not only intimidate Job but to silence him as a means to produce a desperation in Job that would force him to concede to Bildad's way of thinking.

---

[25] Matthew 7:1-4

This method is a type of coercion, but this technique is not new when it comes to the bullies of the world. Coercion is a type of mental torture and is the world's method of separating those who are half-hearted in what they believe from those who are resolved to stand for what they know is true. The bullies of the world realize that the ignorant, the half-hearted, and the foolish will quickly give way to pressure, while those who remain true will prove to be worthy opponents in the end. Such tactics may get people to comply outwardly, but the fickle prove untrustworthy and for the many that surrender to such tactics, they inwardly continue to hold on to what they truly believe, while growing in contempt towards the bully who is exposing the ineptness of their inner character.

Job turned the table on Bildad and asked him how long would he vex, torment, and try to break and crush him with his words. He went on to reveal how his companions' accusations had made them strange to him. He was no longer certain who they were and they had become completely unrecognizable to him. Job counted the times his friends had reproached him. "Reproach" means to wound, taunt, insult, shame, and hurt. In Job's estimation they had reproached him ten times. He again reiterated the faith he had in God. If there was any error in him, God would have made it known to him.[26]

This is clearly a point of great faith on Job's part. As judge, man can always find something that does not meet with his approval and pronounce cruel judgment on the defendant. As a jury, he can be nudged, bribed, and wore down to come into agreement with the disagreeable just to "get along." However, Job was not about to compromise his character to get along with the "self-appointed" judges that implied that God surely had overthrown him and compassed him with a net, nor was he about

---

[26] Job 19:2-6

to be pushed into a false way to get the "oppressive" jury off his back.[27]

One of the reasons for Bildad's attitude is brought out in Job 18:3. Job's unwillingness to agree with his companions and his disapproval of their handling of the matter was interpreted by Bildad as counting them nothing more than vile beasts. Bildad was somewhat exaggerating Job's response, but it became a source of insult to him that justified his attitude towards Job.

He went on to accuse Job's response of being that of anger instead of lamentation, confusion, betrayal, and frustration. Remember that Bildad implied that Job was exaggerating his plight, but we see that Bildad used exaggeration in relationship to Job's response.

Bildad asked Job if his anger would receive any response. Would the earth shake at his logic or the rocks be moved from their foundation of truth? This was indeed a snide remark.[28] Job was not demanding answers, rather he was seeking them. He was not being driven by anger, but was in complete despair due to lamentations that came out of great anguish and sorrow.

Job did not demand that God answer him, but because of his relationship with Him, he lived in expectation that He would help him make sense out of what seemed absurd. Instead of Bildad discerning that Job's response was a matter of faith, he took it as someone who was living in denial as to what seemed obvious to a rational man such as himself.

Job was simply standing on what he knew to be true but he wanted to know if there was anything amiss in his relationship with God, in his character, or his conduct. As a man of faith, he had confidence that God would show him because he had sought Him.

---

[27] Job 19:5-12
[28] Job 18:4

Clearly, what had become confusing to Job was not whether he was in sin, but rather as to why God remained silent and didn't confirm Job's faith, and as a just Judge vindicate him. Job was willing to be exposed and overthrown by God if sin was the reason for his plight. He had also cried against the events that had ravaged his life and for justice to prevail, but he was met with silence.[29]

For Job, God's silence was a two-sided coin. On the one side of the coin was the comforting fact that there was no conviction of sin, but on the other side was the sovereignty of God. Job even made reference to this in Job 19:8.

On the side of the coin representing God's sovereignty, it remained unseen, unturned, and formidable. It was shrouded by the darkness of the unknown and until the light penetrated the darkness to part the unknown, God's silence would have to serve as an answer. Job desired some response from God, but he knew better than to try to tread into that which was only for God to know because it could prove to be dreadful.

God's silence had also left him in a state where it seemed he was stripped of his testimony and the crown that represented his right standing in the Lord and his authority. As a result, he felt like he was broken down on every side, deprived of the hope of ever really knowing the "whys" behind his plight or being affirmed in the faith he was holding onto.[30]

Author Bob Sorge wrote of his Job experience in three of his books. He pointed out that God would not answer Job at his most desperate time; rather, as in the different cases of many saints, He uses delayed answers to prayer to break the saints open, to empty everything that is not of Him and soften the soil of their hearts with tears. It was clear that Job was being brought to places

---

[29] Job 19:7
[30] Job 19:8-10

of brokenness that would require him to let go of all religious notions and give up everything of this world in order to take hold with both hands the thin cord of faith that kept him from being completely consumed by what was happening.

To Bildad the evidence was there to back him up in his conclusions that Job was on the wrong side of God as he made reference to those things that had already happened to Job. He pointed out that the light of the wicked shall be put out in the tabernacle of his spirit and the spark of life will be absent from his soul. Such an individual will lose his strength and he will be tripped up by the net developed by his own counsel, proving to be a personal snare to him that was laid for him in the way he was walking. All of his undertakings will prove to be an exercise in futility. As a result, fear shall beset him and become his ruler. His strength shall be eaten away and destruction will be ready on all sides to devour him. Any confidence he had about his standing before God would be rooted out as he would be brought to face the king of terror, where the brimstone will fall upon his habitation and all his roots will be dried up beneath him and all remaining branches cut off. In the end, there will be no remembrance of him and his name, for both will perish from this earth. He will not have no heirs to carry on any legacy, and those who follow him will be astonished as to what happened to him because he did not know God.[31]

Job admitted that all appearances implied that his companions were right. It seemed that God's anger was kindled against him and that heaven had risen up and encamped around him as if to wait the orders of his destruction. It was as if he stood alone because his brethren were far from him, his kinfolks were not there

---

[31] Job 18:5-21

for him, his acquaintances had become strange to him and his friends forsaken him.[32]

Job admitted that his physical plight caused many to react negatively to him. Keep in mind, their responses had nothing to do with his moral character but with his outward appearance. The maids of his household would not respond to him, his servants did not answer him, and his breath was strange to his wife. Children despised him and spoke against him, and as proven in the case of his companions, his friends abhorred him and those whom he loved turned against him.[33]

Job described his physical condition, followed by these words in Job 19:21 and 22, "Have pity upon me, have pity upon me, O ye my friends; for the hand of God hath touched me. Why do ye persecute me as God, and are not satisfied with my flesh?" To Job it appeared as if the hand of God touched him instead of holding or guiding him, and he was asking his friends to have pity on him. And, since it appeared God had His hand on Job, why did they think it necessary to persecute him seeing that even his flesh was being consumed and that the root of the matter was found in him and not in the Lord?

The problem with man is that when he serves as judge, his pride will never be satisfied with the consequences. Pride has an insatiable appetite, and executing judgment once, no matter how fair and complete it might be, will never be enough to this cruel tyrant. If death is the sentence, pride wants to see the person resurrected and punished some more. If restitution is made, it will see it as a bribe more than a means to make amends and will continue to cry foul. In fact, like our pride, hell is a place of judgment that continues to enlarge its borders. It is where the

---

[32] Job19:11-15
[33] Job 19:16-19

ruined soul is being endlessly consumed by torments that will never be satisfied.[34]

Job wanted his words to be written down, printed in a book, graven with an iron pen and carved in a rock forever.[35] You might wonder why he wanted his words to be a matter of record. The reason is that in the end he would be found to be right. He was not afraid of his words being used against him by heaven, afraid that they would be used as a record against him in any righteous court, or ever misconstrued once their truth was established.

Little did Job realize that his words would be recorded in the most famous and popular book of all time as an ongoing record of the darkest time in his life and the great faith in an immutable God that sustained him. The great wrestling match of his faith would be read about and reread by generation after generation. His life and words would become a matter of great debate, always revealing that man's logic is limited, his reasoning often tainted, and his conclusions wrong. Job's life would expose the great debacle in man's attempt to explain God's sovereignty according to circumstances, identify His will based on limited theology, and define the path of a saint according to prejudicial opinions.

The truth of the matter is that Job's faith would rise up each time out of the debris of accusations, desperation, and hopelessness to always take flight on the wings of hope in expectation of what was promised, but the companions of Job failed to discern and recognize it. They stuck to their narrow narrative, not to ensure the salvaging of a struggling soul, not to encourage a confused mind until clarity once again came, and not to bear up the arms of one who was weary and overwhelmed, but to be exalted as being right in their haughty narratives, confident

---

[34] Isaiah 5:14; 66:24; Matthew 8:12; 10:28; 13:42; Mark 9:42-48
[35] Job 19:23,24,28

in their arrogant arguments, and sure in their overrated conclusions.

However, Job would always come out on top of the argument, not because he was better in his debate skills, but because he always landed on what was true and eternal. He would always land on what he knew was so about God.

To me, the next words that Job spoke summarized the air beneath his slagging wings of hope that would always cause his faith to reach the heights of assurance. These words never serve as a final epitaph of a great man who would not let go of God; rather, they became a living memorial of a man of great faith that would rise up and stand upright in assurance of his great God.

Living faith will never be carved on some stone; rather, it will always become a memorial that points to a great cloud of witnesses that still lives because the faith of saints was and continues to be based on the one true God of heaven. In due time, the Creator will bring forth all of His promises. Those who put all their trust in God and His promises will never be ashamed of having such faith towards God because they are assured of inheriting all the promises. Their words and deeds will be recorded in a book that lives and serves as the very bread and meat to the soul. The words of Job's testimony live today because Job chose to believe and declare the one great expectation the saint possesses.

Now let us meditate on Job's words in Job 19:25-27,

> For I know *that* my redeemer liveth, and *that* he shall stand at the latter *day* upon the earth: And *though* after my skin *worms* destroy this *body*, yet in my flesh shall I see God: Whom I shall see for myself, and mine eyes shall behold, and not another; *though* my reins be consumed within me.

Job's statement is that of faith. Notice how he says, "I know." What did he know? He knew his redeemer, the one who owns his very soul LIVES, and that on the latter day, the last day upon the earth when his body is finally put off for the worms to render to dust, he will SEE HIS GOD for himself as his eyes behold Him alone, even as his outer man that is of this world, ceases to be, his inner being will become transformed.

What doctrine is Job pointing to? that of resurrection. Job believed that he would be resurrected in a different state that would allow him to see God for who He is. In fact, he was confident of the promise. Unlike the Sadducees who debated the Pharisees about whether there would be such a resurrection, there was no wavering or doubt in Job that one day he would inherit this incredible promise. [36] King David believed in resurrection as well. In Psalm 17:15 he stated, "As for me, I will behold thy face in righteousness: I shall be satisfied, when I awake, with thy likeness."

The prophet Daniel spoke of it in Daniel 12:1-3. He talked about a time of trouble as never experienced before, and that God's people whose name is found written in the book of life will be delivered. He then goes on to say this,

> And many of them that sleep in the dust of the earth shall awake, some to everlasting life, and some to shame *and* everlasting contempt. And they that be wise shall shine as the brightness of the firmament; and they that turn many to righteousness as the stars for ever and ever.

Now we can question, what is the essence of resurrection? Jesus stated in John 11:25 and 26, "I am the resurrection, and the life." In John 5:24-29, the Lord talked about the time when the dead shall hear His voice, and they shall live. He told the hearers not to marvel at it for the hour is coming that those who are in the graves shall hear his voice, "And shall come forth; they that have

---

[36] Matthew 22:23-32; Hebrew 6:1,2

done good unto the resurrection of life; and they that have done evil, unto the resurrection of damnation."

The Apostle Paul summarized the importance of believing the doctrine of resurrection in 1 Corinthians 15:12, 14, 21,

Now if Christ be preached that he rose from the dead, how say some among you that there is no resurrection of the dead?...And if Christ be not risen, then is our preaching vain, and our faith is also vain...For since by man came death, by man came also the resurrection of the dead.

In Revelation 20:4, we are told that those who do not received the mark of the beast will live and reign with Christ a thousand years. John then goes on to make this statement in Revelation 20:5-6,

But the rest of the dead lived not again until the thousand years were finished. This is the first resurrection. Blessed and holy is he that hath part in the first resurrection: on such the second death hath no power, but they shall be priests of God and of Christ, and shall reign with him a thousand years.

What an incredible promise Job believed in. Here is the oldest book of the Bible where the man stood on this promise of resurrection with great confidence that he would see his God. The beauty of this expectation is he got to see God before his death. As already pointed out, Job saw God at the end of this challenging journey.

This is probably why Job ends his defense with a warning in Job 18:29 that was directed at his companions. The warning is that they should be afraid of the wrath that will bring the judgments of the sword upon them, pointing to the fact they would know it was a matter of the judgment of God leveled at them.

Keep in mind, to accredit God with the move of the enemy is to blaspheme, and to falsely accuse one of God's saints requires

163

Him to one day vindicate that person, while bringing like judgment leveled at the innocent against the accuser. When we think we are right about a religious matter according to self-righteousness, we can see ourselves becoming a mouthpiece for God. When we are passionate about our religious point of view, we can become a cruel judge that perceives we are defending God's character while stripping the innocent of any recourse. And, when we become stiff-necked about a religious opinion, there will be no place of reasoning where reality can be inserted into the narrative to take away any personal blinders.

As Christians, we must remember it is easy to judge the Jobs of the world, but when we do, we must keep in mind that we have not been touched in the same way and we are limited by worldly logic that does not enlighten us, but blinds us to what is true and eternal.

The End of the Matter
(Job 25)

Bildad had used all the evidence of circumstances to reveal what he thought to be an air-tight prosecution against Job in his first two discourses, but it was all circumstantial evidence. He had even coerced him, but Job made it clear, even in his last response to his three companions, that he would not let them remove his integrity from him so they could be justified in their own eyes. He had an assurance that in the end, after he was weighed in the just balance of God, that his integrity would be clearly known.[37]

There was no proof Job had sinned in the darkness or that he was toying with some iniquity. However, Bildad was not willing to let Job have the last word in the matter. It was obvious that in spite of riding high on what each companion perceived to be the

---

[37] Job 27:5; 31:6

elevated waves of rationalization of the situation, they were hitting the rugged shoreline of truth. The problem was they were blinded to the truth and arrogant in their conclusions which would not allow them to surrender to any other conclusion than the one they were maintaining. As a result, they kept insisting that their personal interpretation and evaluation of the matter was true and right.

Job was not staying down with each punch they leveled at him. In fact, it seemed as if he was becoming bolder in his declarations about his integrity and his faith towards God. This boldness made him appear more arrogant in his claims to them, when all Job was doing was stating facts that were known to them. His companions made it sound as if Job's account was a ruse to cover up that he was justifying himself for some sin instead of honoring God with a sign of brokenness and confession.

Regardless of what angle they came from, how clever, or diplomatic their presentations were, Job was not accepting the cases that his former friends brought out in the courtroom of logic. He clung to the Rock, while holding up truth and becoming bolder in his faith, as his spirit found assurance in what he knew to be so.

Bildad would present the last discourse of Job's three companions. It would be a short discourse because each previous presentation hit an immovable wall that left all three of them frustrated and sulky which no doubt created a blanket of resentful silence.

When you consider the length of the discourse, you realize it was the last shot taken against Job by these three men. The last shot represents a type of morbid resignation that will not honorably or quietly go down without trying one more time to hit the target. For Bildad it was the feeble attempt of declaring that those aboard the sinking ship were still on the right side even though victory seemed to be presently eluding them.

Bildad would fit nicely in that group who believes if you say something long enough and with enough passion, people will believe it. It is true you can fool some of the people some of the time, but not all of the people all of the time. There comes a time that when all but the truth will be left standing while all false, tyrannical, and skeptical conclusions will be shattered into unredeemable pieces.

You have to keep in mind this last shot was taken at Job because of his last response to Eliphaz who implied Job was exalting himself above God because he would not agree with their evaluations. Job clearly refuted such a slanderous notion.

Bildad had three final questions to ask in his concluding presentation. He began with God.[38] This is a good place to begin, but it was not to exalt God, but to set the record straight about Job. It was not to lift up the truth of a matter to bring clarity, but as previously stated, to take one last shot at Job.

Bildad pointed out the obvious that all dominion belongs to God and only He can make peace in high places. It is amazing that Bildad almost hit the target as to where this real battle started. He nearly got beyond his small elevated spot to see into the eternal.

He admitted there is no way to number the Lord's armies or predict who His light will arise on. [39] There was clearly a clash going on because God had put a light on Job, but even Bildad implied that it was hard to predict who and when God will highlight such a person. His implication, in a way, hit the target.

Bildad used the concept of "predicting" as to where God's light will arise on someone, and pointed out that it was close to impossible to identify such a person, but as believers, we have a responsibility to discern such a person once the light does rest on His servant.[40]

---

[38] Job 25:2
[39] Job 25:3
[40] 1 Corinthians 2:11-15; 1 Thessalonians 5:12,13

It is from this premise that Bildad asked two of his questions in Job 25:4, "How then can man be justified with God? or how can he be clean *that is* born of a woman? "Once again Job's defense of his faith had nothing to do with justifying himself at the expense of God's righteous reputation. He never implied that he had won God's approval through personal merits; rather, he believed God, and his faith in God determined his actions which were considered reasonable to him and not meritorious.

Job had clearly established early on that he was born of woman and no doubt knew that Adam's fallen inherent disposition had been passed down to all of his seed.[41] There was no place where Job implied that he was without sin, but he did believe he stood upright before the Lord because his motives were pure and his attitude correct.

To confirm his position, Bildad reminded Job in Job 25:5 that the moon had no brightness compared to God and that the stars were not pure in the sight of God. It is hard to say what point Bildad was really trying to make. First of all, the moon has no light, it simply reflects the light of the sun. This is true for man. It is the life in him that becomes the light that is reflected through the mirror of his soul (eyes) and his outward countenance. We know that the only true light is God and if His life is not in the person, there will be no real light to speak of.[42]

Job knew he possessed the breath of God, and said as much in Job 27:3. He knew his life was the life God had given him. Perhaps Bildad's point was that his light was like the moon that has no real light to reflect, which implied he had no real life except a preconceived notion of one born out of his own imagination.

The light of the stars is not pure because there are various sources of gases that determine the heat and light that is given

---

[41] Romans 5:12-14
[42] Matthew 6:22-23; John 1:1-5

off. God is the source of true light and it is pure and transparent. Perhaps Bildad was implying that Job's so-called "light" (life) was like the unpredictable gases of the stars that give the impression of emitting pure light, but it is a light that is not consistent and obviously contaminated.

This is why Job's response in Job chapters 26-31 dealt a lot with creation from the makeup of the universe with its numerous stars and planets to the function of the earth we live in. It was Job's way to show he understood what Bildad was implying and took him to task to silence any misconstrued implications, false accusations, and slanders. Job clearly understood that even though creation is incredible, it was never meant to outshine the Creator. All of God's creation was to speak of His majesty, to point out His great power, and to confirm His existence, but it was never meant to be worshipped or used in any way as a comparison to the Creator.

This brings us to Bildad's final question, "How much less man, *that is* a worm? and the son of man, *which is* a worm?" (Job 25:6). Because of sin, man in a sense, has been brought to the lowest place spiritually in God's creation. Jesus became lower than the created angels when He became man.[43]

Creation is subject to laws and beasts to instincts, but man, who was initially given dominion over the earth, is the greatest slave of all. He is a slave to his lustful appetites, his vain imaginations, and his perverted logic. He has been put on the auction block of the world to serve decadent despots, bow before cruel tyrants, and taste the bitter whips of harsh taskmasters.[44]

Bildad was trying to put Job in his place by knocking him off of what he perceived to be an arrogant pinnacle by reminding him he was nothing more than a worm, but he was unsuccessful,

---

[43] Hebrews 2:6-10
[44] Romans 1:20-21; 7:14

because Job knew in spite of everything, he was standing on the Rock of God.

Being compared to a worm is not an insult to a righteous man. The truth is we will all be rendered into the same status as a worm. Consider this prophetical reference to our dear wonderful Lord and Savior Jesus Christ in Psalm 22:5-8,

> They cried unto thee, and were delivered: they trusted in thee, and were not confounded. But I *am* a worm, and no man; a reproach of men, and despised of the people. All they that see me laugh me to scorn: they shoot out the lip, they shake the head, *saying*, He trusted on the LORD *that* he would deliver him: let him deliver him, seeing he delighted in him.

Jesus in His humanity became as a worm. He seemed like He was subject to every power and whim around Him. But He allowed Himself to be brought to such a humble state for an important mission: to pay the ransom for the souls of mankind.

Worms are pitiful creatures. They are defenseless, subject to every circumstance, predator, and obstacle. The best they can do is crawl when threatened, squirm in the jaws of predators, and try to find cover in the darkness of the earth to keep from being destroyed, while accepting their ultimate fate to become consumed, regurgitated, and left as residue in the earth or dried up on some man-made surface.

Even though worms are the lowest as far as creation, they are of the utmost importance because they serve as food. They actually ensure an environment where seeds can take root in fertile ground prepared by them, to ensure the ongoing process of life that produces valuable results.

Worms often represent the state of humility and Job certainly had been brought to such a place. Circumstances had caused him to fall to the lowest point of the Rock. He had been broken at the base of the Rock by an unbearable darkness, while being crushed

169

by a rockslide of accusing and slanderous boulders. His faith was shaken, his soul tattered, and his spirit wounded, but he continued to cling to the Rock because even in the darkness it remained the only hope he had left, a hope that never failed him in the past.

The great debate had shaken him mightily, forcing him to cling even tighter to what he knew about the Rock, while the accusations caused him to come to the end of himself to know that the eternal Rock was the only answer, and slander had made him stand up and grab the Rock while the grave darkness tried to consume him as he waited for the dawning of the light. He knew the light would eventually come, either in his present life or in the one promised him. He used each indictment leveled against him as a foothold of faith to climb that sturdy Rock, each time establishing his footing on a higher and more secure place.

Job was the one who opened the door to this debate and he would be the one that would end it where his three companions were concerned. He opened the door because he started with his plight, but he would end it with the reality of God, but not before he exposed Bildad's character in Job 26:2-4.

Consider what he asked Bildad,

How have you helped him that is without power? How have you enabled those with no strength? In what way has your counsel displayed true wisdom and how is it you can declare things you know nothing of? Where has your insight come from and whose spirit was inspiring you?

Job's questions revealed that Bildad had failed in every area in Job's case, as well as when it came to others. It is from this premise that Job spoke of something that we like to ignore in Job 26:5 and 6: hell. Those who are dead (in sin) and the inhabitants of the grave are now trembling in the bowels of the earth and why? Because hell is laid naked before the Lord and there is no covering as to the destruction that is taking place.

He speaks of God's greatness as revealed in creation in Job 26:7-13. He pointed out in Job 26:14, the functions of creation are part of the Creator's way of doing that which is in line with His order, but Job reiterated how little is heard of His workings, but even if man heard, how many would understand?

Job 27:1 and 29:1 tells us this part of Job's discourse was a parable. I have already mentioned that Job 26:5-31:40 is one long parable. This parable speaks of God's ways in creation, wisdom, and workings. When it comes to wisdom, the Jews lay claim to the book of Proverbs and Christians to the book of James, but the presentation of true wisdom has been given to all mankind by Job.

Job's presentation of wisdom gives us much insight into man's understanding of creation. God is the sum of all true wisdom; therefore, lasting wisdom comes from above.[45] In both wisdom and the parables man can observe contrasts that can be weighed in a just and reasonable manner. It is for this reason there can't be just balances in justice without wisdom present to bring discretion and distinction to the different sides.

Wisdom has contrasts in order to bring explanation and instruction, but parables contain the element of the mysterious in order to bring awe and wonderment to a person as he or she ponders and seeks precious gems in clear, but deep, waters. Job's presentation of wisdom holds that one incredible mysterious element of God intact: His sovereignty.

Divine wisdom is behind all that has been created. Creation functions according to unseen laws that maintain working order in a vast universe that produces awe. God in His sovereignty has displayed incredible designs in His creation that causes man to ponder that which proves to be beyond explanation. He has provided unseen treasures that inspire man to go deeper or climb

[45] James 3:17,18

higher, along with dimensions that stirs up the curiosity of man to explore beyond his limited scope of understanding.

Job brings these incredible realities out in a wonderful presentation of wisdom, while revealing the source of it. We are told in Hebrews 11:3 that through faith we understand that the worlds were framed by the Word of God, so that things that are seen can be accredited to our invisible Creator. Remember, it is the unseen things of creation that verifies the existence and workings of the Godhead.[46]

In Job 28:12, Job asked where shall wisdom be found and where is the place of understanding? After all, man cannot know the price of wisdom because it is too great and its origins can't be found among the living because it is beyond any comprehension. As each part of creation admits that such wisdom can't be found in its depths, or gained with priceless gems, or obtained from great heights, Job made it clear that God is the only one who understands the ways of wisdom. But, how does man reach into the rich vein of heaven and gain the heights to develop true discretion and discernment in order to possess its nuggets?[47] Consider what Job said in Job 28:28, "And unto man he said, Behold, the fear of the Lord, that *is* wisdom; and to depart from evil *is* understanding."

Job pointed out that the reason he walked the way he did before his great God, was because he feared Him. When you properly fear someone, you do not want to break their heart or your heart by displeasing them. Fear of the Lord is an attitude that possesses respect that desires to honor the Lord in acceptable service and conduct. It possesses an awe that wants all responses to become a form of worship worthy of God, and counted as being acceptable to Him.

---

[46] Romans 1:20
[47] Job 28:14-27

Fear of the Lord enabled Job to obtain wisdom from above, but departing from evil brought a greater understanding to him about God's character. Fear of God taught him the honorable way, while refusing to be part of evil, and fleeing from it, always put him on the path of righteousness. His righteous acts were never done to become a point of exaltation for him, but because it was his reasonable service to the God he was in awe of and worshipped. Heavenly wisdom also allotted him the discretion to know that the integrity of his faith would not let him do any less than that which was right.

In the discourse that followed in Job 27-31, Job waded in and out of the greatness and justice of God to find himself in the wrestling match with the whys behind his plight. He spoke of God's justice and his knowledge of the ways of righteousness when it came to his own life.

We see him longing for the time that the presence and light of God highlighted his walk and activities. Blessings abounded, his family was about him, and everywhere he went, he sensed God's incredible grace upon his life. He brought relief, comfort, protection, and joy to others, and as a result was respected by those at the gate of his community.

However, due to his present state, that had all changed. It was heartbreaking and unbearable. His body bore the crushing reality of his circumstances, but his great struggle was not the loss of status among those of his community; rather, it was because God was shrouded in the dark shadows of silence. If he could be assured that he had not stepped in a wrong way, or allowed the ways of the world to trip him up or subtly been taken captive by riches, or was unknowingly bowing to some strange idol. He struggled with it because he had demanded the ways of righteousness from himself to the point that he made a covenant with his eyes not to lust after a woman, or let his tongue be unbridled to speak in ignorance or frustration, nor did he let his heart be secretly enticed to give way to the idolatrous affections and infatuations of others.

Even though it appeared that he was cast down by the cruelest of events to never rise again, he still knew God held his days in his hand, and that one day death would claim his body, but he would be appointed to the house of the living.[48]

This was the reality of Job's faith. He was wrestling with the present, while remembering the life he had in the past with God. It was his faith that allowed him to settle for the unfairness of the present long enough to stand confident in light of a glorious future.

Job was willing to face the truth of the matter. If he had covered any transgression or hid any iniquity as Adam did, he would clearly humble himself and repent, but the silence of heaven was loud and had become tormenting at times. It was true God's silence left him without conviction, but he also was lacking any recourse to settle the matter.[49]

He desired to know if any offense was being held against him, but God had not pointed any out and the fruits of his life did not bear witness to any such discrepancy. His companions could accuse him all they wanted, but until God spoke to confirm the matter one way or the other, Job had to stand his ground to maintain the sanity of his own faith.

Job did not have anything left except his inner integrity and his faith towards God. He had been stripped of everything of value in the physical world, but his integrity would not let him agree with his companion's dark interpretations and conclusions about his circumstances, and his faith would not let him let go of the light of God that still existed in his heart and soul.

Heaven had been silent, but at this point every rabbit trail, every possibility, every angle had been breached, as well as the

---

[48] Job 30:23
[49] Job 31:33

last shot fired over the Job's bow, and now his companions could do nothing more than be silent like the heavens.

In his last discourse, Job had started with God, pointed to God, wrestled before God, and all that was left for him to do was end his words as he continued to faithfully stand on what he knew about God. He would also wait quietly in the silence, while maintaining his inner integrity to resist any surrender to darkness or resignation to silence the foul claims of hypocrisy, self-righteousness, and outward show of so-called "self-righteous indignation." [50]

---

[50] Job 31:40

11

Traditions
(Job 11)

Surface understanding produces
fragile devotion.
(Unknown)

Zophar is somewhat of an enigma. As already pointed out, there is no one man or group of people that he can be identified to. He had a history, but other than what was recorded in Job, there is no other record in existence.

Since man is known among a circle of people, his attempt to leave a personal mark of uniqueness is often based on family and cultural influences. As man gains a reality check, he realizes that he is not the only duck in the pond, for there are others who also think their existence is important and unique. When he realizes that his circle is small compared to the world of people, he has a unique opportunity to become more realistic about what will truly count in the end, but such realism can also drive him into an insipid world of scoffing, indifference, anger, or insanity. The final reality, when it comes to this world, is that unless he is among those with power, he will never be among the elite, and if some record is left, it will be recorded in a historical event where all remembrance of him as a person will be swallowed up by the immensity of what was happening.

Zophar's name is recorded because of Job, but his record represents much of mankind. The history of many civilizations is missing, buried by the sands of time, revealing that the importance of man is based on relationships and not positions, and the test of man is a matter of inner character and not his recorded opinions.

As believers, we realize that unless our history goes back to Jesus and the cross, we will become like a Zophar where our life becomes an enigma, at best recorded on some family tree that never began with us and will not end with us. If our relationships with others are not honorable, our reputation will quickly become buried by foul, confusing feelings and if we are void of having a relationship with God, there will be no record of a legacy to be found or an inheritance that we can be identified too.

Thus far in this great debate, we have had Eliphaz the dreamer who based his presentation on an experience he had that he diplomatically transposed onto Job but became a scorner and desperate when Job would not bow his will to it. We then had Bildad, the pious philosopher who proved to be an indifferent bully with his questions and platitudes that never reached the depths of Job's sorrows or the heights of truth. These two companions backed both their cases up with their theology surrounding God to bring about credibility to their presentations.

Man knows he has no credibility standing alone. He must be part of the in-crowd to feel justified in ignoring or crucifying the truth, while tacking God on wherever he can to verify his conclusions as being true. This is the only way for man to have any real confidence and assurance that he is on the right side of history, making his life noteworthy and his legacy enduring. Clearly, time, days, and death will remind man that his time is short, his earthly legacy temporary, his worldly importance a matter of opinion, and his limited influence a simple flash in the pan that dissipates quickly, to never be seen again.

Zophar was part of the group and in agreement with his companions. Because of his position of being part of the group and the fact he was in agreement with the other two probably gave him a certain confidence about the case being presented against Job. Each of their arguments seemed as if they hit the same target, but from different directions.

These companions of Job fought fiercely to be right, only to be told in the end that they were wrong. Zophar's recorded discourse is nothing but a flash in the pan, set ablaze by an appearance of indignation that spoke of being intellectually insulted, irritated of what was considered to be a moot point to him. In fact, his attitude was bordered on boredom, but on behalf of traditions and God, he took issue with Job.

In order to put someone in their place, you must designate a place that has been established and considered reliable. In Zophar, the place had to do with traditions that were passed down.

Man is often comfortable with traditions because they have been established by those of past generations, passed down as part of a legacy to ensure order and identity, and propped up by noble attitudes and actions of piousness. As a result, many perceive that traditions are a worthy cause and this was true in Jesus' day.

The Pharisees perceived their traditions, (their oral laws) were right and it became their cause to promote them as they appointed themselves both the conscience and authority to ensure the Jewish people would adhere to them. However, Jesus told them that their traditions nullified the authority of God's commandments. Later He called them hypocrites who were nothing more than whitewashed tombs with decaying, dead bones of religion encased in them.[1]

---

[1] Matthew 15:1-9; 23:1-35

Like the Pharisees of Jesus' day, Zophar was going to bombast Job by coming out of the gate swinging with sarcastic accusations. "Bombast" is ranting that covers up the reality that the person who is doing it can't really respond to the issue at hand. Ranting is a way of talking over your opponent to avoid listening to them so in the end you believe you have silenced them when in reality you have become deaf by drowning them out with rhetoric.

In Zophar's first statement he informed Job that all of his words would not justify him. Job was not speaking for the sake of speaking, he was presenting a very detailed defense, but Zophar did not want to hear it. However, Zophar did hear it because he called him a liar and accused him of mocking the truth. How did Zophar come up with such conclusions? because the three of them could not make Job ashamed.[2]

Man shames, Satan condemns, and the Holy Spirit convicts. Shame shuts down a soul as it insists on making one bow, while Satan's condemnation makes man hopeless because there is no place of recourse to seek deliverance. The Holy Spirit convicts in order to cause man to respond in true repentance to seek God's favor, faith to receive forgiveness, and hope of complete restoration.

Job challenged them to plead with him based on something legitimate by withdrawing their severe hand of judgment from him and then he would expose himself to examination. For them to be fair in their examination, they would first have to cast aside all preconceived notions and judgments so that they could truly hear what he was saying. He wanted them to present him with credible indictments so he could make peace before his death.[3]

---

[2] Job 11:2,3
[3] Job 13:17-23

The problem with man when he shames man as a means to get him to bow to a narrative contrary to his spirit and will, is that he becomes a poor substitute for the Holy Spirit in that individual's life. Such an individual tries to prick the conscience of the person, as a means to shame him or her for thinking outside of his particular box of thinking. It is for this reason that Job asked Zophar if he was contending for God. Job also wisely asked him if he would like to be searched out in like manner, and in the end discover that he was mocking God as if His ways and judgments were that of mere man.[4]

Zophar accused Job of saying to himself that his doctrine was pure and that he was clean in his own eyes. Once again, Job's defense was not based on just his doctrine but on the fruits his actions had produced, and he never declared that he was clean. It is true that man's ways are clean in his own eyes, but Job's defense was based on the fact that God had not convicted him of any transgression committed against commandments or iniquity of character. And when challenged to present him with the list of his sins and iniquities, they had nothing but vain speculations.[5]

Doctrine is often associated with religious practices or rituals that are based on the traditions passed down. We do not know exactly what the doctrine consists of that Zophar is mentioning here, but we are told that man's doctrine leavens God's pure doctrine and puts terrible burdens on others. As believers, we know real doctrine comes from God and will end in a person doing His will. We also know that if a person does not abide in the doctrine of Christ, they are not of God.[6]

For Zophar, his ranting displayed an attitude of dignifying himself that was propelled forth by the emotion of righteous

---

[4] Job 13:7-9
[5] Job 11:4; Proverbs 16:2
[6] Proverbs 4:2; Matthew 16:10-12; John 7:16,17; Hebrews 13:9; 2 John 2:9-11; Revelation 2:24

indignation. In his indignation, he appealed to God to back up his position. I am sure that like James and John who wanted to call fire down from heaven in the incident in Luke 9:52-56, that Zophar would had been told by the Lord that he was operating in a wrong spirit. From this premise Zophar asked Job why would God disclose such wisdom to him because it was obvious that there was a side that was hidden from him and that he was not getting what he deserved.

Job assured Zophar that he had been mocked by his neighbors, but he also stated that he had called upon God and He had answered him, but God's answers matter little because the righteous man is laughed to scorn by those who do not believe. It is here that Job refers to himself as a righteous man, not based on his works, but on his standing before the Lord. He stood by faith and the Bible is clear such faith is accounted for righteousness.[7]

To Job, it appeared that his companions were implying that he was sitting back in ease without any understanding during this trying time. However, they were the ones who appeared to be waiting for the righteous, such as himself, to slip as evidence there was some type of folly in their midst.[8]

At this time Job is speaking from an attitude of annoyance and is not accepting his companion's irrational conclusions. In each case, they had many words and cemented conclusions based on theology, but they lacked any wisdom to address his plight. Zophar's appeal to God in Job 11:5 and 6 caused Job to conclude that in this man's logic his circumstances actually showed God blesses the robbers of the tabernacle and secures those who provoke Him.[9] Once again, we see Zophar's real attitude towards Job based on circumstances and not reality.

---

[7] Job 12:4; Romans 4:2,3
[8] Job 12:4,5
[9] Job 12:6

Zophar then asked Job how could he think for one moment that he could possibly know the height and depths of God for He is as high as heaven and deeper than hell. He goes on to state that His measure is longer than earth and broader than the sea. He will cut off and shut up, or gather together those whom He will; therefore, who can hinder Him?[10]

Job would not debate Zophar's claims about God's operating from great heights and is not limited by depths, but he counteracts Zophar's attitude towards him by asking if wisdom stopped or would die with him. He stated more than once that he was not inferior to him. Job made it clear that he had understanding just like Zophar. After all, who could personally know the matters that have been touching his personal life? He brings out the fact that the beasts, the fowls, the earth and the fishes can teach or declare matters of God to mankind. All of creation praises the Lord except some people. Keep in mind, Jesus pointed to creation as a means to instruct and inspire men in His teachings.[11]

In Job 11:11-14 we see where Zophar admitted that he thought Job to be a vain man and that God could not regard him. His advice to Job, was although he was born like the colt of an ass, it would be wise for him to prepare his heart and stretch out his hand towards God, and if iniquity be in his hand to put it far away and not let it dwell any longer in his tabernacle. Again, we see how these companions of Job would not accept, consider, or concede that Job had a life before, and in, the God of the universe that they had no real knowledge of.

Job in his discourse made it clear that his great desire was to speak to the Lord for it seemed as if His face was hidden from Him, and that it appeared as if he was now an enemy of God who did not deserve any audience with Him. If His hand was upon Him,

---

[10] Job 11:7-10
[11] Job 12:3, 7,8; Job 13:2; Psalm 148; Matthew 6:25-30

he wanted to make peace with Him so he no longer had to live in dread but could die in peace. It was his greatest desire to reason with the Lord about any existence of such iniquity, transgression, and sin in his life, but it was becoming clear that he had to simply trust Him in His silence.[12]

In his response to Zophar, he asked a very important question in Job 12:9, "Who knoweth not in all these that the hand of the LORD hath wrought this?" This is an incredible question! Consider what Job was saying, "How do you know the Lord is behind all of these things?" Job asked the Lord why in His providence He was allowing these things to happen, but he never accredited them to Him.

This bit of information is so vital, but it can be easily missed. Once again, we see that Job understood that his situation was not about God's disapproval of some sin in his life, but something that had greater significance behind it, but it was shrouded in the mysterious providence of God. He could have not known that God was using his faith as a great witness, a testimony that a righteous man in the worst of times will always choose to love, believe, and worship his Creator because He is worthy of such pure sacrifice.

We must keep in mind the presentations of Job's companions were not based on the truth of God, but their misguided desire to defend or honor His reputation. Job called them forgers of lies and physicians of no value and stated that with God's strength and wisdom, the deceiver is His to do with and judge. He is the One who leads counsellors into desolation and will make judges into fools for He is the one who sets up leaders and nations as well as brings them down. He takes away the heart of the chief to rule, causing them to wander while groping and staggering in the darkness. Clearly, God exalts and humbles who He will and does not need man to speak on His behalf in defense of His reputation.

---

[12] Job 13:3, 22-24

Job asked Zophar if he spoke wickedly or talked deceitfully for God.[13]

These three men's presentations came down to them putting their theology before truth, and when religious people do this it will cause them to tell a lie in order for reality to fit into their present point of view. Job's defense was not a matter of putting God's character on trial, but stating the reality of his plight.

Job followed up his question with the understanding of God as Creator, that He alone has brought forth all matters. Each of our souls are in His hand along with the breath of mankind. We have been given the means to hear and taste things as well as develop wisdom and understanding through years of experiences, but the counsel of all wisdom and understanding along with sustaining strength is His alone. Once God decides to break something down or shut it up, man can't build it up again. He is the One who withholds waters and dries them up and He knows the deep things of darkness and brings forth that which lingers in the shadow of death to the light.[14]

Zophar ended his presentation with the fact that the eyes of the wicked shall fail and they will not escape for they have no real sustaining hope. Clearly, he tried to leave off his discourse in Job 11:13-19 on a positive note by declaring that if Job adheres to his counsel, then he can steadfastly lift up his face without fear as he forgets his misery and simply remembers it as waters that passed away. His strength will return and everything will make sense and he will be secured once again in hope as he finds rest for his soul. He told Job that none would make him afraid again, and people would once again seek his favor. However, Zophar's feeble attempt just showed that he had no clue as to where Job was.

---

[13] Job 12:16-25; Job 13:4,7,8
[14] Job 12:10-15, 22

There are some interesting statements here. Zophar acknowledges that Job was confused about his state. He makes reference to the type of respect he had before his ordeal. He also admitted that Job would not have to be afraid again, but there is a total divorcement from the depth of Job's loss and sorrow.

Job is far from being divorced or closed down to man's plight. He has a handle on the reality of man. We especially see this reality coming out in Job 13:25-14. In wrestling before the Lord, Job asked if the Lord would break a leaf already cut from the source and was being driven to and fro, as well as pursue dry stubble that had already been separated. It was as if the sins of his youth were being used against him.

This was all quite confusing to Job because he acknowledged that the Lord had disciplined his steps in the past to walk down designated paths according to what was ordained, but his body was decaying like a rotten thing and like a garment that was being moth-eaten.[15]

Job acknowledged that man is born of a woman, his time is short and full of trouble. He comes forth as a beautiful creation, only to be cut down to never be seen again on earth.[16] It is in Job 14:3 he asks the Lord if He was going to look upon one whose life is a vapor and bring him into judgment in his vulnerability without a cause.

Job knew the answer, but that does not stop the inner debate when the outer debate is loud and accusing. Sometimes the inner debate has to be verbalized to highlight that the case has already been presented.

When you consider Job's case, you will realize that he was asking God to consider his frame. Man is born into a state of

---

[15] Job 13:28
[16] Job 14:1,2

spiritual poverty, with his days numbered and his time of death appointed.[17]

Unlike a tree that is cut down, but can be once again brought forth, when man's life ceases, he will not rise again in this life. Job wanted to be hid in the grave until the deep waters of trouble and wrath passed over him and after a set time, be remembered by his Creator and called forth. Job knew even in his present situation that he would wait all the days of his appointed time until the change came.

We again see that by faith Job was waiting for the Lord to call and he would answer him, knowing he would come forth. It would be at that time the Lord would see the type of work that He had performed in him.

In Job 14:18-21 Job makes it quite clear that which affects man's existence, does not shake, change, or disrupt God in His plans and ways. Creation is in constant flux. Mountains falling amount to nothing and rocks that are removed are often worn down by other elements. Rebellious man may try to prevail against God at every turn only to find God does not change and they are the ones who will be brought low in the end. However, the one aspect of man that never changes is that his flesh shall have pain and his soul will mourn within.

We have considered Job's statements that reveal his confidence in God. This confidence is a matter of Job's faith. The Apostle Paul referred to the law of faith in Romans 3:27. The law of faith begins with one believing God as to what is true. It graduates from believing to walking in what is so and then it reaches heights of abiding in the assurance of His unchanging character, the heavenly promises, and eternal glory.

Job struggled with his plight to come into line with the law of faith by believing that his GOD IS. There is nothing more you can

---

[17] Job 14:4,5

take away from or add to the equation. All things begin with God, all things are under God's providence, and all things will end with God.

It is because Job could land on who GOD IS that he could make this statement, confidently knowing God holds the reins of all matters. This famous statement has been used by many in the greatest times of testing, "Though he slay me, yet will I trust in him: but I will maintain mine own ways before him" (Job 13:15).

It looked as if God was bent on destroying Job, but Job knew that the Lord was his salvation. He made a couple of declarations. One is that he will maintain or defend his ways before God. Job was not saying that his ways made him acceptable to God, but keep in mind, he was being accused of some transgression or some hidden iniquity. He was very aware that his integrity was intact and he had not committed such an offense; therefore, he was able to present a sound defense.[18]

The second thing he said is that he had ordered his cause. This points to the fact that Job already presented his case in order to receive the proper judgment call whether it be a penalty or vindication. We clearly get an insight into Job's presentation in Job 14, and Job already knew the verdict.

Remember how Zophar asked Job how he could regard himself as being justified? Consider the verdict Job knew he would receive, "I know that I shall be justified" (Job 13:18). Justification has to do with pardon, forgiveness, or a state where no complaint, accusation, or offense can be brought against a person because all sins of the past are covered for they have been properly addressed.

Consider what Job said about sin in Job 14:16-17. He stated that the Lord knew all of his sin but his transgression was sealed

---

[18] Job 13:15-18

in a bag and his iniquity sewed up. The only ones drawing out the trial against Job were his companions.

In spite of his companions' accusations, Job knew he would ultimately stand justified before God, not because of his upright lifestyle or actions, but because of his faith. When one operates according to the law of faith, he is always a candidate to stand justified in the end. The Apostle Paul put it this way, "Therefore we conclude that a man is justified by faith without the deeds of the law" (Romans 3:28).

Disdain
(Job 20)

At this point of the debate, it had become more intense with neither side budging. Opinions had become more cemented into place, while genuine faith was being challenged to withstand the onslaught of unwarranted accusations, while its capacity was enlarged to climb above the rotten debris of slander that were flung from every angle.

At this point Job made some profound statements that showed his faith, revealed his inner life, and maintained his integrity. It was becoming obvious that he would not be moved from what he knew was true about his God, regardless of the so-called "facts" of what had been established, evidence of present circumstances, and Job's unwillingness to bend and bow.

Job had brought no accusation against God, but his unwillingness to bend towards the logic of his companions and bow before their conclusions implied that he was leaving his Creator holding the bag for his unfair plight. They all knew God was sovereign and nothing could bypass Him without Him allowing it. In the minds of his companions, Job had to be guilty of some sin or God was guilty of being unfair and unjust. Their theology would not allow such a notion to be alluded to or entertained. They could see no other scenario except that Job was guilty of some flagrant sin that had somehow been hidden but was now being exposed by his plight.

Each case of prosecution caused Job to cling tighter to what he knew was true and sure. The fiery test of his faith proved that untested faith remains surface, unrefined faith proves weak, and unenlarged faith will shrivel up and be taken away by the next great wind of trials.

We come to Zophar's second and last presentation. He tried to speak with some dignity and civility, but it was obvious that he was void of all real discernment. His approach was to try to disguise the fact that he was about to strip Job of his dignity. Even though his presentation was the same as his previous one, it had a different twist and flavor to it.

In his last presentation he was willing to take "prisoners," as the saying goes, but in this one he had no intention of taking any prisoner. Remember, this debate seemed to border on pure boredom to him, and he had no desire to see it continue on. Perhaps in his mind, he perceived he would put the last and final nail in the debate by an all-out frontal attack on Job's character.

The appearance of trite dignity in people like Zophar towards the Jobs of the world is nothing more than a disguise to hide utter disdain. In such disdain, diplomacy is dropped, logic is no more, reasoning is past, and what is left are what are considered the raw facts of the matter.

Zophar begins his presentation by stating that he must make haste to give an account of his disdain for Job and the reason for it is because the reproach or shame that has been leveled against him by Job.[19]

---

[19] Job 20:2,3

Job's unwillingness to accept his companions' conclusion and his audacity to expose the misery they have heaped upon his own soul through their ridiculous judgments did not leave them in a good light, even in their own eyes. It was for this reason Job called them "miserable comforters."[20]

Zophar was not willing to bear any such reproach. After all, he and his companions were simply trying to help Job see the error of his ways, and call him to repent so that he could be restored. What was so bad about such attempts? However, they failed to see that God will never strip the worst of sinners of their dignity, nor will He leave them in a state of misery. What leaves people in a state of misery is their unwillingness to address sin, turn to God, and repent, so He can restore them.

He claimed that the spirit of understanding caused him to answer. Zophar was "so far" from understanding the real crux of the matter. Understanding is what you must seek out, but it can only be rightfully interpreted by wisdom from above. Ephesians 1:17 and 18 talks about how the Spirit of wisdom and revelation enlightens our eyes to understand. You can't understand the unseen without the Holy Spirit revealing it to your spirit.[21]

Zophar verified what he was about to say, as not going back to God, but back to the fact it has been so from the beginning of man's existence in the Garden of Eden.[22] Again, we see reference to the tradition of the old being passed down as being the gauge of what is true.

This is where Zophar goes right into the judgment of the wicked. His triumph will be short and the joy of the hypocrite will be for a moment, and even though the likes of him reaches great heights he will perish like dung and those who knew him will ask, "Where is he?" Zophar went on to say that the wicked will fly away

---

[20] Job 16:2
[21] Job 20:3; 1 Corinthians 2:11-14
[22] Job 20:4

as a dream to never be found again and when there is any mention of him, it shall be chased away as a vision of the night. No eye will ever see him and no place shall mark his existence.[23]

Zophar was correct about the end of the wicked, but this was the indictment he was leveling at Job. Job understood that very fact. As his own defense attorney, he asked if he could be heard without being discarded and allowed to present his full case before being mocked.[24] Clearly, Job experienced mockery before, during, and at the end of his presentations.

Job clarified that he was not making his complaint to man. Lamenting and vexing over a matter is also not complaining to God, showing unbelief, or being bitter. Job's spirit was rightfully troubled, and so would anyone else in his same situation. It was not up to his companions to take up God's cause at such times because they lacked perspective and understanding. Job wanted them to rightfully mark or honestly look at him for they would be astonished at his plight and they would lay their hand on their mouth and cease to speak in utter ignorance of his plight.[25]

Eventually, each point of debate will strip away all false pretenses to expose the spirit and agenda behind a man. Oswald Chambers refers to this point as a "Primal Clash" where each party gets down to the foundation of a matter.

It is interesting to point out that Zophar was trying to undermine Job's righteous acts of service to others as being nothing more than fleeting moments of joy and triumph for him, and ultimately, they would prove to be nothing more than dung. His reputation would fly away and any mention of his name would be treated more like a byword, rather than a blessing.[26]

---

[23] Job 20:5-9
[24] Job 21:2,3
[25] Job 21:4,5
[26] Job 20:6-9

Zophar told of how the children of the wicked would be oppressed by the poor and they would in turn obtain ill-gotten gain. Zophar was implying that Job gained his wealth from ill-gotten gains and not blessings. Remember how Job said that it seemed as if he was being indicted for the sins of his youth? Zophar implied that the sins of his youth still remained with him and as a result his strength had failed him and his words would be considered poison to others. The "ill-gained" riches he had received would be vomited up and the Lord would cast them out of his stomach and he would then partake of its poisonous fruit and die.[27]

In mentioning the wicked, Job remembered certain matters about them which caused him to become afraid and tremble in his flesh. We know the reason for Job's repulsive response towards wickedness is because he feared God and eschewed evil. Job brings out that the wicked and their offspring can live long lives, seem at peace, play hard, sing loud, experience prosperity in this world and go to the grave in peace; therefore, the abundance of blessings or the lack thereof was not an indicator of a person's spiritual condition.[28]

Man's spiritual condition comes down to his attitude towards his Creator and his relationship with Him. Job said of the wicked that they say unto the Lord, "Depart from us; for we desire not the knowledge of thy ways. What is the Almighty, that we should serve him? and what profit should we have, if we pray unto him?" (Job 21:14,15). It is for this reason Job made a point to declare that there is no good in the hand of the wicked to receive anything of worth, and that their counsel was far from him.[29]

Zophar pulled out all of his punches to wake Job up to his "miserable" state. He believed that his indictment was correct

---

[27] Job 13:26; 20:10-16
[28] Job 21:6-13
[29] Job 21:16

even though it was contrary to what he already knew about Job. He used general terms to describe the wicked, and it was obvious that he was pointing an accusing finger at Job. He made it quite clear that whatever the wicked obtained it would become lost to them because they had oppressed and forsaken the poor and violently taken away their houses. Such people can't feel quietness in their inner part and sense they can't save that which they desire. There will be no meat left for them and it will become obvious that in spite of previous self-sufficiency, the wicked will find themselves in dire straits and those in their same league will turn on them.[30]

This companion of Job was implying all of Job's outward deeds were a cover up to hide his real contrary works of darkness. In his summary, Job was nothing more than a hypocrite. What Job claimed was opposite of what he said and did. There was nothing real, pure, or sincere in him, but Job would not receive such implications from Zophar. He told him that he knew his thoughts and the devices which he had wrongfully imagined against him.[31]

It is important to point out that being called a hypocrite is a great offense to a righteous person. In a way it would be like calling them a fool. In our society hypocrites abound. Actors once were called hypocrites because they portrayed themselves to be something they were not. A person who did not keep their word was considered a hypocrite because they presented themselves in a way to con others as to their real intentions. They are accepted frauds who present a false reality, especially in the name of entertainment. Hypocrites were clearly for entertainment purposes, and could not be entrusted with the real matters of life. They might be considered good court jesters in the halls of kings, but would not be considered trusted advisers, and yet how much

[30] Job 20:17-22
[31] Job 20:27

of our present-day reality is being established by nothing more than hypocrites, acting out on the different stages of the world which includes in the pulpits and in the halls of Congress.

Due to the fallen disposition, we will all find ourselves to be hypocrites at different times. It is not because we intend to entertain, con, deceive, or act some part out to throw people off as to what is really going on, it is because we easily deceive ourselves about our character, intentions, and abilities. Our intentions are often impulsive because they are driven by emotions and not integrity. We may want to do right, but it eludes us because we discover that we were not realistic and sober about what it would take to see a matter through. And ultimately, we often discover we do not have the means to complete something we have impulsively agreed to do. It is for this reason that the Apostle Paul cried out, "O wretched man that I am! Who shall deliver me from the body of this death?" (Roman 7:24).

However, there are people who are practicing hypocrites. Their way is false, their presentation is deceptive, and their hands ready to do mischief to carry out their deeds. This is why Jesus stated our words should be aye and nay because past the reality of a simple answer proves to be sin.[32]

Zophar was not done with reiterating his point. Keep in mind Job lost everything and the presentations of these men were in light of that very fact. After bringing imagined accusations against Job, Zophar told him that when a wicked man is ready to eat of his ill-gotten gain, God's wrath will fall on him. Heaven will reveal his iniquity and the earth will rise up against him. Even if the wicked man manages to get away, he will be chased down by other means such as the iron weapon and the bow until the arrow brings him down, piercing his innermost being. Every treasure the wicked lays up will be met with misfortune and devoured by God's

---

[32] Matthew 5:37

wrath, leaving bitterness behind. This is the portion appointed to him by God.[33]

Job could agree with Zophar about the end of the wicked. He made it clear that the candle of the wicked would be put out. He compared them to stubble that would be picked up with the wind and driven like chaff. It was true that the children of the wicked followed in the ways of their family's iniquity and as a result they likewise would see God's destruction and wrath. Like all mankind, the wicked will eventually die and be covered with worms to be remembered no more. They are reserved to the day of destruction and will be brought forth to the day of wrath. No one will be able to defend them and in light of the grave, the clods of the valley shall seem sweet to them, but sadly many have, and will, walk the same path of death and destruction.[34]

Job clearly understood the ways of the wicked and their end, but it was his way of telling Zophar that he would never have any part in the ways of the wicked. His final statement to Zophar is very revealing. Zophar thought himself to be wise and possessing the truth about Job, but Job's statement in Job 21:34 revealed the foolishness of his conclusions, "How then comfort ye me in vain, seeing in your answers there remaineth falsehood?"

---

[33] Job 20:23-29
[34] Job 21:17-33

12

The Upstart
(Job 32-37)

*One of the tests that many of the great saints have
shared is to suffer a negative reputation—to have others who
love and serve God decide that you're suffering because
God's displeasure is upon you.*
(Bob Sorge)

When I have discussed the book of Job in the past, there were those who were surprised that there was an actual fourth man that had come with Job's companions. By the time they get to this fourth individual, many see the debate as redundant and fail to note that Elihu is not Eliphaz.

Elihu's name means "God He is, the Lord He is, or Jehovah He is."[1] This individual was sitting under the radar during the debate because he implied that he had simply come to observe. One can only gather that he was interested in theological and philosophical matters and wanted to see how the elders handled it. As elders they had a responsibility to teach wisdom to younger men due to the experience behind them, but Elihu was upset with his companions because according to his calculations, they had failed to present a viable case that had justified God in casting down Job.[2]

---

[1] Original Meaning of Scriptural Names, Compiled and © 1949 by Lucy Bates
[2] Job 32:2-7, 12; 35:16

This is an important insight into how this observer graded the participation of Job's companions. Like his companions, he perceived that Job's words were void of knowledge, useless, foolish, and lacked real wisdom, and even classified him as answering like a wicked man. Elihu felt that the other three companions had failed to present a credible case and even admitted that Job stumped them in the end. His conclusion was that Job had left the other three men amazed so they were unable to answer him, but Job had not addressed him.[3]

As we will see, Elihu used the same points as his companions to convict Job, and even made mention of Eliphaz's case, which was based on a dream by mentioning that the Lord will speak in visions when one is asleep. He felt since he was an observer that he had not allowed himself to be influenced by any partiality and he would avoid trying to flatter Job in any way. In other words, he saw any compliment or acknowledgment about Job's character and deed on the part of the other three companions as being a form of flattery and not truth.[4]

It is hard to know how many of these men came to Job with an argument somewhat formulated in their mind about what was going on with their friend. We know they were shocked and overwhelmed when they first saw him and sat with him seven days without saying a word. Once again, we don't know if any of them formulated their conclusions during that time or simply confirmed and reinforced what they suspected to be the case during the silent period.

There are a couple of things we know about Elihu: 1) he was young and did not feel the freedom to speak, 2) he agreed with the conclusions of Job's companions, and 3) he did not personally know Job. However, even though he admitted up front that what

---

[3] Job 32:14-17
[4] Job 32:6,10,14-17, 21,22; 34:35,36

he was about to speak was his opinion, and as we will see, Elihu, in his arrogance, concluded that he knew the very mind of God concerning the matter at hand with Job. He also perceived that he possessed the necessary wisdom to put the three companions who failed to sway Job to shame, while silencing Job with so-called "wisdom" he could not refute.[5] Clearly, there is a big difference between man's mere opinion and God's voice of truth.

Unlike the other three companions, who spoke in defense of God as if He was their client in the court room of reasoning, ever defending His character, Elihu actually claimed to be the voice of God who would instruct these elders in the ways of wisdom. In fact, he declared that he would fetch knowledge from afar and would ascribe the righteousness to his Maker because his words would not be found to be false and that the One who is perfect would be present to confirm them.[6]

Keep in mind Job had finished his discourse. He may have started with his plight and lamented over it at different times, but he always landed on the reality of God. He may have wrestled before God, but he chose to trust what he knew about God and held to the enduring promises of heaven. He ended his discourse at the safest place and on the most reliable source to all matters: God's great wisdom that works through every arena of His sovereignty.

Job never sought his companions' pity, but he did desire their compassion. He needed sounding boards to bare his heart, be honest about his struggles, and have someone weep with him in his sorrow instead of using his plight to carve out judgmental boards that would be used to hit him over the head with nails of accusations and spikes of slander firmly embedded in them.

---

[5] Job 32:3-12, 17; 33:3,4; 34:35
[6] Job 32:10,17-20; 36:2-4

There are different ways people react to being challenged when they have become cemented in their opinions. They not only perceive they are right, but they must come out of the debate as being justified in their rightness. The need for such justification has to do with pride.

There are those, like Eliphaz, who will climb on top of you with any religious measure and experience available in order to be right, while others will use your plight or challenges as a personal elevated point to step on top of you and over you with great scoffing like Bildad. There are others who, like Zophar, will use disdain to pound you into submission in order to create a mound upon which they can step and tout that they are right. Finally, there are those like Elihu, who in ignorance, passionately mount up on some unseen pinnacle of arrogance so they can look down on you while attempting to ground you into insignificant dust.

When I consider Elihu, I am reminded of another individual who was nothing more than a conceited upstart. In youthful zeal this individual thought self to be quite wise. This person saw self as being knowledgeable about the matters of God, right in the stands they took, and infallible while standing on pinnacles of opinions. That person was me.

I was a new Christian, still young in years (21), silly in my notions, and immature in character. I had much to learn, but I thought I pretty well knew what I needed to know after reading and studying the Bible through a few times. Each opinion became a pinnacle, each judgment a foothold in my ascending zenith, and each conclusion a leg up to the next ledge carved in by conceit.

I assumed the view from my narrow pinnacle of conceit confirmed my perspective and I presumed I was right since I couldn't see anyone else who even could touch what I considered to be the wisdom behind my conclusions. Even though I did not stand alone in my all of my conclusions, I did stand alone in my arrogance.

I look back at that time in my life and shake my head at the arrogance that exalted a novice into a place of expertise and authority, while dishing out judgments in regard to people and theology. The Bible warns against giving such novices any real platform because as I learned, it will feed the arrogance of foolishness, producing a blind monster of ridiculousness that is bound to walk off the cliff of embarrassment and absurdity, to finally end up in the bottom of the pit of depression and defeat.[7]

As previously stated, Elihu agreed with the three companions, but was angry at them because they had failed miserably to convince Job of what he could see as being obvious. In his mind, he devised the approach he could use to convince this "obstinate" person about the real source behind his plight, thereby, ensuring that God would be justified in His dealings with Job. It was clear that he perceived Job's defense was a means of declaring that he was more righteous than God.[8] As we will see, he used Job's case against him by bringing in the contrast that would leave this poor, abused saint guilty and silent.

Elihu recognized he would be a mere instrument of God, but he claimed his ear was towards Him; therefore, he would speak on his behalf. In fact, he stated his words possessed knowledge and that he was compelled to speak, had to speak because it was inspired by the very breath of the Spirit in him, and that he would speak upright words. These words would not bring terror or great pressure on Job to outwardly comply while vehemently disagreeing within his being. It was also clear as he got further into his presentation that he became more convinced that he was God's voice and that the others must give ear to him and hear his words. He even asked them to bear with him a bit longer for he had something to stay on God's behalf.[9]

---

[7] 1 Timothy 3:6
[8] Job 35:2
[9] Job 32;18,19; 33:2-7, 33; 34:2-4, 16, 34; 36:2

Part of Elihu's strategy was to assure Job that his words were taken to heart because he clearly heard what he was saying. At one point he even instructed Job to hearken to him while holding his peace and allow him to speak, and if he had anything to say afterwards to do so, for he desired to justify him, as if he had any real authority to declare Job justified. If not, Job needed to listen to him and he would teach him wisdom.[10]

Again, we must remember that God was not behind Job's plight and was not in need of any defense. If He did speak it would not be through an arrogant young man, for He resists such pride. Job already stated that he knew he stood justified because in essence there was no inward conviction of the Spirit. Jesus was very clear in Luke 8:18 that we must beware of how we hear a matter because the same way we measure out judgment onto others it will be measured out in the same way to us.[11]

If opinions are already formed, people will naturally judge all matters according to their opinions, no matter how impartial they perceive themselves to be. They may avoid flattering a person while presenting their case, but their conceit will end up flattering them into a type of delusional arrogance as to how wise they think they are as to their knowledge and advice. It is for this reason Paul told believers not to be wise in their own conceits.[12]

In order to confirm to Job that he had heard his words, he presented a summary of his case. However, what we will see is that the summary is based on how Elihu perceived Job's case according to his own understanding. He simply took Job's words and fit them into his conclusions, which changed not only the meaning of Job's presentation, but its ultimate intent or the spirit of it. Elihu's summary would reveal an attitude of autocratic

---

[10] Job 33:31-33
[11] Job 13:18; 1 Peter 5:5-9
[12] Romans 12:16

authority that was clearly riddled with biases, assumptions, and misconstrued conclusions.

The first thing he perceived Job as saying is that he was clean of all transgression, innocent of causing any real offense and completely void of iniquity. There is no place where Job made any such claims. Man is plagued with both the outward battle of avoiding the traps of transgressions and the inward battle of iniquity where they must depart from any temptation that would cause the "old man" in them to rise once again and start influencing the attitudes and steps of a person. Job was clear early in the debate that he would be perverse in making such claims and that his three companions knew he was not wicked.[13]

This novice would continue to hammer Job with statements that made him appear as a delusional religious person who lived in complete denial of what was right and true about his situation. According to Elihu, Job had declared he would not lie about himself. A man who has integrity need not make such a declaration, for his upright reputation would confirm such a fact. Elihu perceived Job as saying he had no hope for his plight was incurable, when in reality Job only declared that he was not guilty of transgression at that time and stood justified.[14]

Elihu pointed out that Job thought he was actually missing God's righteous judgment on earth, and that his cause was before the Lord and that he was waiting for an answer. This was true, but Elihu inserted his conclusion by stating that this was not so for God had answered him by visiting his anger on him, but Job didn't recognize it even though it was extreme. Unlike Bildad, at least Elihu was acknowledging that Job's process had been extreme.[15]

He also declared that Job stated that it does not profit a man to delight himself with God and consent to Him and that his

---

[13] Job 9:20,21; 10:7; 33:9
[14] Job 34:5,6
[15] Job 35:14,15

complaining was a form of iniquity. He went on to say that Job had continued to add rebellion to his sins in a mocking fashion as he multiplied his words against God, which revealed how Elihu perceived Job's presentation of his plight. In his apparent "delusion" of justifying himself, Elihu was implying that Job was claiming he was more just than God, and asked him what can he give God and what can God receive from him. To bring comparison, Elihu asked when does one have a right to say to a king that he is wicked or a prince that he is ungodly.[16]

The comparisons that Elihu used are important to note because to confirm his case, Elihu used how God deals with the righteous and wicked. He rightly stated that God's eyes are upon everyone and there is no place of darkness and shadows in which man can hide iniquity. He is mighty in power and understanding, and does not ignore the trivial, nor will He hear that which originates with vanity, but His eyes are upon the righteous, and He will set them up as kings, forever exalted on the throne. The Lord will justly consider man and from there the person will enter into judgment. Elihu then goes on to make reference to mighty men, which implied that in the height of his influence in the community, Job was considered a "mighty man." [17]

According to Elihu God will overturn the mighty man's works in the night and destroy them. He actually breaks the mighty man and their works into pieces without having to make any enquiry about them because such men turn aside from Him and will not consider His ways. In fact, such men will cause the cries of the poor and afflicted to reach heaven. We know that Job was well known for his acts of charity and intervention, but Elihu even had an answer for Job's acts by stating that the hypocrite can only reign because the people have been ensnared by them. In other

---

[16] Job 34:5-7,18,37; 35:2, 7,8; 36:21
[17] Job 34:21-23

words, Job's acts were all a show, a ruse and the people he had helped had been taken captive by them to keep them from really seeing the character of his inner man.[18]

The idea that his deeds were just an act, pointed to Job as being a hypocrite. This label Elihu used freely at different times and the reason why is because he felt he knew what was in Job's heart. He made a statement that in the hypocrite's heart they heap up wrath and they fail to cry out to the Lord when He binds them with cords of affliction, and for most they will die in their youth and their life will be left unclean. He also stated that even if Job was a hypocrite, the Lord would have moved him out of a strait place into a broad place to partake of a table of abundance. His conclusion as to why the Lord had not done this is because Job was full of the judgment of the wicked.[19]

Since Job was such a hypocrite, it was easy for Elihu to attach the term "wicked" to him. The one earmark of the wicked that sets them apart is how they treat the poor. The wicked cause the poor and afflicted to cry, but the Lord will deliver them and open the ears of the oppressed.[20]

Elihu had clearly misjudged an innocent man, but he could do so with conviction because he did not know Job. It is also important to point out a contradiction where Elihu stated that God will overturn the mighty man's works in the night, but stated that He strikes the mighty man like he does the wicked in the open where others can see it because such an individual has turned aside from Him and will not consider His ways.[21]

It is pointed out by Elihu how God's eyes are upon all men and He sees their steps. He will not do wickedness or commit iniquity and there is no partiality in His dealing with man for He is just in

---

[18] Job 34:22-28,30
[19] Job 36:13-17
[20] Job 34:28; 36:15
[21] Job 34:27,28, 30

all He does when it comes to judging the deeds and ways of man. God will often let adversity happen to bring man's soul back from the pit and to once again be enlightened with the light of the living. This is all true, but Elihu was falsely accrediting what was happening to Job as being punishment from God and trying to bring his soul back from the abyss. He implied that Job was experiencing the fetter of adversity and was being held by cords of affliction in order to reveal his wickedness that found its basis in pride. It was God's way of opening his ears to the discipline taking place so he could hear his command to return from his iniquity. Elihu was right, that God will try to contend with man in his wickedness and that eventually He will pay man according to His deeds, but He will not pervert justice, and before His wrath falls, He will use whatever measure He must to bring man back from the ways of death to the land of the living.[22]

There was a point where Elihu almost seemed like he was pleading with Job to not let God's wrath reside upon him, opening him up to be enticed into scorning his chastisement. He must avoid letting his suffering cause him to turn aside so that he has to be ransomed.[23]

This upstart used Job's plight to show him he had to be guilty. In his mind, God's silence was due to the sin of pride and self-sufficiency that avoided any and all judgments, and that such a person will be chastened with great pain upon his bed. He spoke of this person's flesh being consumed for it is marked to perish, and that continual strife was in his bones to the point he no longer would desire food or life as he drew nearer to the grave where his body would return to dust. Clearly, he was callously describing Job's plight, but his judgmental arrogance caused him to swing out even further on the limb of absurdity by stating that in the night

---

[22] Job 33:29,30; 34:10-12, 20,21; 36:8-19
[23] Job 36:18

Job must have desired people to be cut off from the land of the living. In short Job's great plight was revealing the depth of Job's so-called "wicked character and evil state."[24]

Elihu stated that the Lord had found occasion against Job and counted him as an enemy and he later asked, if it is possible for an enemy to govern and condemn the One who is Just and Mighty? He described Job as a man who drinks up derision like water, while keeping company with workers of iniquity and walking with the wicked men.[25] As pointed out through the debate, as a righteous man, Job had no problem being found guilty, but not by men who were limited in their understanding, but by God who knew all things and would be just in His judgments.

Like the other three men, Elihu encouraged Job to stop complaining about his plight, accept his afflictions as being part of his punishment by taking full responsibility for his sin so that he could truly repent. Elihu pointed out the great benefits of Job repenting. If he repented, God would send him a daysman or intercessor to stand between him and God. Once He was forgiven, he would be restored in his body and his strength would return. It is upon such restoration that he can again pray to God, knowing that grace awaits him and joy will rise up when he begins to see his Creator's face. At that time, he will confess his sins to others, and admit that he perverted what was right and testify that wicked ways will not profit a soul. Job was promised that the Lord would deliver such a repentant soul from going into the pit and that if he obeys and serves Him, he will spend his days in prosperity and pleasure and not perish and die without possessing the real knowledge behind his plight.[26]

At one point the upstart warned Job not to rely on past riches and his former strength to keep him from God's wrath. Elihu made

---

[24] Job 33:17-22; 36:20,21
[25] Job 33:9-13; 34:7-9, 17
[26] Job 33:23-28

it clear that it was right for Job to say he was being chastised and that he will no longer offend God, and give him permission to teach him what has been hidden and that ultimately God will recompense everyone, whether they refuse to submit or agree with Him.[27]

It is interesting to note how Elihu ended his discourse. He ends it with God and His mighty workings in creation. He reminded Job of what he knew to be true about God and to hearken to their examples and stand still while considering the wondrous works of God. After all God is the one who judges and gives in abundance. He is righteous, great and His ways unsearchable and no creature can anticipate His insertion into creation's workings.

He admitted that what troubled his heart was the thundering from heaven and the power behind the elements that can move mountains. Keep in mind, he was a young man, but what he expounded about God in Job 36:22-37 and His mighty works in creation is very impressive. He talked about the water cycle, the making of clouds, lightning, thunder, snow, whirlwind (tornadoes), and the cold out of the north where the great waters are frozen. It is God who causes the storms to come whether it is for correction or to show mercy.

It is God's mighty voice that goes forth through His creation in excellency and He will not allow those who oppose Him to stand. He commands all the workings of creation. He determines the weight of the clouds and balances them out, for He is perfect in knowledge. He has spread out the sky revealing that His majesty is awesome.

Elihu pointed out that the Almighty can't be really explained for He is excellent in power, judgment, and justice. He also maintained that He will not afflict, and even though man may fear Him, He does not show favoritism to those who are wise of heart.

---

[27] Job 34:31-33; 36:11-12; Job 36:19

For a man who declared that he would explain and point out to Job God's attitude, he was pretty much contradicting himself at the end of his discourse. Perhaps he was even becoming a bit confused.

It was clear that these four companions understood aspects about God, but they could not really explain His part in Job's situation. In their attempt to do so, they ended up accrediting their Creator with something He was not behind and falsely accusing an innocent man of something he was not guilty of.

Man, in his limited sphere of understanding can arrogantly take much for granted about the unseen world. In order to justify his understanding, he can hide behind what he thinks he knows about God, use what he does know concerning God as a point of confirmation, and stand on mounds of arrogance as he touts his expertise of God. Sadly, in the end, he not only will misrepresent Him, but he will miss seeing Him in a matter altogether.

Elihu would end with God being just, but in his presentation of God he had put Him in a twisted box in order to justify his indifferent attitude and harsh judgments towards Job. It seemed that Elihu did succeed in bringing the debate to a close, but coming to the end of human reasoning does not make you the victor.

For Job, it would have been a waste of time to try and reason with Elihu. He no doubt remained unconvinced, and it would have been a moot point to start the same defense all over again. It was clear that the young upstart had his mind made up and he had concluded that Job's presentation was wrought with wicked claims about his plight, evil intentions of covering up some grave sin at the expense of God's reputation, and that he was worthy of being afflicted; therefore, in his mind God remained just.

It was obvious that no matter what Job would say, his defense would be used against him. The question is, did Elihu win the debate after demeaning Job, misconstruing his presentation, and declaring him a hypocrite? Let me say many debates end in a stalemate resulting in some type of default where everyone walks away with the same opinions still intact. If there is any real victor, it is the person who, with the last word, settles the matter with truth.

13

The Final Word
(Job 38-39)

*I have found that even during those times
when the path is the darkest, he leaves
little bits of evidence all along the way—bread
crumbs of grace—that can give me what
I need to take the next step. But I can only
find them if I choose to SEE.
(Mary Beth Chapman)*

When you walk with Job through his long valley of great loss and despair, encounter the tremendous bumps of personal doubts and challenges with him, endure the blowing winds of accusations, withstand the endless rhetoric of logic, taste the bitterness of indifference, and come to the very end of it to only encounter the looming pinnacle of arrogance, you are ready to say "ENOUGH IS ENOUGH!"

Walking with Job has taught me a lot about human reasoning, especially when it comes to my own personal reasoning with its limitations. When I first read the book of Job, I started out admiring his integrity and faith, but I found myself confused by the logic of the different presentations only to see glimpses of light breaking through the darkness when Job's faith took center stage.

It was my desire to understand, to see what I needed to learn from Job that allowed me to catch glimpses of a man who left an incredible witness behind. The book of Job answered some basic questions that had loomed before me, but the answers sometimes caused greater questions until I realized there are some things I will never understand in this lifetime. Such matters are meant to be mysterious, shrouded by the infinite, and hidden within the unseen realms of glory. God in His sovereignty has and always will maintain His divine right to withhold matters that are none of my concern, but I always had the assurance that what I needed to know to finish my course would be revealed to me at the right time in the right place.

In the past, when I had finished reading Elihu's scathing presentation, I felt bad that Job didn't have an opportunity to put the upstart in his place, to reveal an even greater dimension to his faith. There are only two ways to stop a debate. The first way is quit feeding it; but for an upstart like Elihu, he would see silence as a victory for him. If it involved some competition, the second way is that a judge would have to step on the scene and declare either the winner or the end of the debate because it is a stalemate. I always felt that Job got slighted when it came to Elihu until Oswald Chambers pointed out a very simple fact in his book, "Baffled to Fight Better."

Consider who stepped on the scene after Elihu's presentation? It was the Judge of all, the Lord of lords. It is important to note that God spoke directly to Job once. It becomes obvious that there is a division being marked between His two presentations, and the question is why is there such a division? It is also important to point out that Job did not respond the first time the Lord spoke, but he did in a short interlude where a question was personally asked Job and God's final presentation.

There is also another point that must be established. Hebrews 1:1 tells us that at sundry times and in divers manners God spoke in time past unto the fathers by the prophets. It is clear that God would only speak to and through one of His prophets. This begs the question. Eliphaz felt the Lord had given him a dream and

Elihu had declared the Lord had shown him wisdom, but who did the Lord speak to, identifying him as the prophet? Job! Who would He speak through to bring forth instruction, admonition, and exhortation to the others? Job!

It is clear that since Job was the prophet among the five men, God would address him, but the question is who was He speaking to? As I said, Job responded in what I refer to as a short interlude and the Lord's second discourse. It is obvious the Lord was speaking to an individual because He instructed him to gird up his loins like a man for He was demanding an answer. Let me ask you, who acted as if he had all the answers? Job admitted he was confused and didn't know what was going on. Who implied he had received wisdom from above to instruct his elders? Who presumed He was speaking on God's behalf and attempted to confirm it by expounding on what he knew about God in light of creation? If God was telling any man to gird up his loins, for He was about to demand an answer from him, it would be the arrogant upstart Elihu.

Let us now consider what transpired where Elihu was concerned. First of all, Elihu stated that God speaks through thunderings and lightnings. In this case God was using a whirlwind, and in the situation of Elijah, He used a small still voice.[1] We must never put God in a box because He will prove that He will never operate within, or according to, man's theological box.

Consider what the Lord asked up front, "Who is this that darkeneth counsel by words without knowledge?" Again, who declared that his words possessed knowledge in Job 33:1-3? Elihu was big on showing how he understood the matters of God by pointing out how the Lord had created all things, something that was clearly understood by the other four men, but the Lord

---

[1] 1 Kings 19:11-12; Job 37:1-5

challenged the depth of his understanding by asking if he was present when He laid the foundations of the world.

It was also true there were things that, like the other four men, Elihu understood about the functioning of the earth, but the Lord asked him if he knew the measurements of the earth, if he could declare the width of it, and who had managed to stretch a line upon it to measure it? He goes on to say who fastened the world in its place and laid its cornerstone? He asked if he was present when the morning stars sang together and the sons of God shouted for joy? [2]

Elihu had talked about the water cycle, but the Lord asked him if he was part of establishing the borders of the sea, and had he entered the springs and searched out the depth of it. Elihu could speak of clouds, but it is the Lord who numbers them, determines the size, shapes, and travel of the clouds. He is the one who weighs them as to the moisture they carry and when and how much they release, and determines the path they will travel. He also spoke of how, out of the womb, comes ice and frost and how the waters form glaciers[3].

And, what about the waves? Well, the Lord determines their path along with the paths that lightning, the wind, rivers, creeks, and rain travel. Elihu may see the sun rising but can he command it and does he determine the path the light will travel to part, expose, and dispel the darkness? He may see the dirt but does he know the exact time it forms a clod? He may see the marvels of the sky, but did he form and put together the Mazzaroth (zodiac)?[4]

In Job 38:21 the Lord answered His own initial question by saying, "How can you know this because you were born?" In a way it appears as if the Lord is being a bit sarcastic when He

[2] Job 38:5-7
[3] Job 38:8-22
[4] Job 38:24-35

follows it with "or because the number of thy days is great?" Remember, Elihu pointed out that he was the youngest in the group, and as Job pointed out at different times, man's life is but for a moment, and yet this upstart saw himself as their instructor. Regardless of the wisdom acquired in one's lifetime, as the Lord pointed out in Job 38:36 He is the one who puts wisdom in the inward parts of man so he can see beyond the physical world and gives understanding in someone's heart so he can properly comprehend. Man can know nothing, is incapable of explaining anything, or gain substantial insight outside of God.

The Lord asks if he, as mere man, could provide food for His creatures. It is important to point out that in Job 38, the Lord talks about heavens, the sky, the cycle and movement of water, but at this point He is about to make a transition from the happening above to His sovereignty when it comes to the creatures of the earth.

The Lord is the designer of all of creation. We can see the outworking of creation, but it is the inworking of it that reveals more about His sovereignty. It appears that some of His creatures defy the laws of the universe. For example, consider the long neck of the giraffe. A mature bull can stand about 18 feet tall in order to reach its food source, but for blood to be pumped up to this animal's brain, it takes a strong heart, which it possesses. There is a challenge in this design because the blood pressure exerted by the heart would actually burst the blood vessels of this creature's brain when it bends down to drink water.[5] However, nothing is too great or impossible for the Designer of the Universe to solve. The Lord put valves in the arteries of the giraffe's neck to

---

[5] Although it can be found in other sources, the information on the unique designs, functions, and instincts of the different creatures mentioned in this chapter was taken from *The Evolution of a Creationist,* © 1994, 2002, 2004 by Dr. Jobe Martin. The information on the giraffe can be found on pgs. 131-134

close as the blood makes its way to the brain to regulate the pressure.

What about the woodpecker who has an industrial-strength beak in order to make a hole in the tree to reach its food source?[6] Can you imagine the pressure the woodpecker exerts in creating that hole? He would have one big headache except the Lord designed this bird with a special cartilage between its head and beak to absorbed the shock, while it opens and closes its eyes between each peck to keep out the sawdust. These birds have unique feet that form a tripod that allows it to stabilize itself on the side of the tree, as well as a tongue that is like a spearhead with a number of barbs of hair on it. The tongue is coated with a sticky blue-liked substance that can capture the insect.

Consider the whale that can withstand the great pressures at the depths of the ocean and the angler fish which lives more than a mile deep in the ocean. On the female head of this fish is a "fishing rod" tipped with an "artificial worm" that dangles like "bait" over her mouth to attract her next meal. However, at this depth it is too dark for the bait to be seen so the Lord put a special kind of light in this false bait as a means to attract her food. This light is made possible by a compound that is oxidized with the help of an enzyme that scientists call Luciferace. The enzyme has been broken down into more than 1,000 proteins.[7]

Again, we are reminded that it is what is not seen by the naked eye that reveals more about our Creator's sovereignty, wisdom and artistic abilities. As I learn about the uniqueness of God's different creatures, I often imagine that He had great pleasure in creating them. It is almost as if He designed something that would end up being a failure just so He could solve the problem of His design with something so simple, yet complex enough to become

---

[6] Ibid, pgs. 265-269
[7] Ibid, pgs. 159-161

profound, bringing child-like awe and wonderment to man as he considers the wisdom and majesty behind each design.

In Job 39, God asked Elihu if he could explain the working of instincts in different creatures. He started with the wild goats and asked if he knew when they delivered their calves and how they knew what to do when it was time for delivery. Take the wild ass who makes his home in a wilderness. He searches for every green thing while avoiding mountain pastures, cities, or coming under some master.[8]

Consider the unicorn which is a two horned wild ox.[9] This ox is strong and is fierce and will not let itself be domesticated like a regular ox.[10] Perhaps that is why Joseph's glory was compared to the horns of the unicorn in Deuteronomy 33:17, because the distinction of his glory, that often proved to be fierce, was evident in his descendants, Ephraim, who was the dominant tribe in the ten tribes of Israel.

The tribe of Ephraim's symbol in the wilderness was that of an ox, but they were considered fierce and refused to be disciplined.[11] The unicorn often turns its head to one side to push back or attack with one horn and maybe that is why Psalm 92:10 declares that like the horn of the unicorn, the Lord will be exalted as the Most High.

The next two creatures that the Lord pointed out in Job 39:13-18 were feathered. Unlike the ostrich, the peacock's feathers are beautiful in presentation, but when the ostrich lifts herself up in flight (run), she even puts the horse to shame. However, the similarities between these two creatures is that they both simply lay their eggs on the ground. The peacock covers her eggs with the dust to warm them, but the ostrich simply lays her eggs in the

---

[8] Job 39:1-8
[9] Smith's Bible Dictionary
[10] Job 39:9-12
[11] Judged 7:24-8:3; 12:1; Psalm 108:8; Hosea 11:3-12

dust and takes off without any regard for them, leaving them vulnerable. However, the Lord put within the male ostrich the instinct to protect the eggs from all wild creatures until they hatch. Perhaps He was giving men the insight into the type of protection they are to provide for their family.

When we talk about some of the male species of certain creatures being responsible for the welfare of their offspring, the Australian Megapode or "incubator bird" would fit in this category. This bird resembles a chicken or small turkey and is often referred to as a brush turkey. All birds use their bodies to incubate their eggs except the ostrich and the Megapode. This bird piles up great heaps of debris that will serve as the incubator. This incubator can be as high as 20 feet and as wide as 50 feet, allowing the female, who first tests and must approve of the nest, to lay 20 to 30 eggs. Along with the warmth of the fermenting compost and other heat sources such as solar heat and volcanic actions, the male Megapode must constantly adjust the nest to keep it at 91 degrees and 99.5% humidity to ensure the eggs hatched. Amazingly, once the chick pecks itself out of the egg (a three-day process) it is ready to fly and live without any assistant from the parents.[12]

It is clear that the Lord was pointing out that as Creator, He sovereignly put within each creature the instincts to reproduce, to forage in whatever environment they live in, to act according to their design, and never really step outside of the order of creation's function. The only part of God creation that steps out of order and causes chaos is man.

The next creature the Lord pointed out is the horse. This animal can appear to be a dichotomy. He has been given a mane that flies in the wind, but he is earth bound to fulfill another destiny. At one point he can revolt at small things while mocking fear when

[12] The Evolution of a Creationist, pgs. 57-60

facing some great battle. The horse makes its own path as it devours the ground with speed and faces off the opposition with fierceness and rage. His nostrils can make him appear formidable, but yet he is sensitive to the reins of his master.[13]

Man may discover what a creature can do, but God in His sovereignty knows the real potential and calling of all creatures. He asks, does the hawk fly according to its own wisdom? How does it know to stretch out his wings towards the south when winter approaches? And, what about the eagle? This bird mounts up and makes her nest on high where she dwells on the high places where she observes all from afar off, ever seeking to provide for her young.[14]

Instincts have ensured the survival of God's creatures through the centuries. An interesting bird to consider is the Pacific Golden Plover. This native of Hawaii flies to Alaska in the summer time to make a nest and fend for its young. As soon as the young can fend for themselves, the adult Pacific Golden Plovers take off for Hawaii, leaving their young behind. The young birds must gain strength and weigh enough on their own to be ready for their long flight to Hawaii. This bird is the size of a pigeon and the average weight for this bird before it leaves Alaska is 200 grams. Keep in mind they must fly miles over an ocean and manage to arrive at the Sandwich Islands, small specks in the Pacific Ocean, and yet within them is the navigation skills to do so. These birds do not swim; therefore, they must fly non-stop for 88 hours, but according to their size and the number of grams they would burn, they can only go as long as 70 hours. On these facts alone, it would be impossible for them to complete their flight, but God put within them the instinct to fly in formation and change leaders on their flight. This rotation in and out breaks the wind, taking less energy

---

[13] Job 39:19-25
[14] Job 39:26-30

on the bird's part and leaving them with 6 grams of fuel left over by the time they reach their destination.[15]

Man has been given a moral conscience and senses to spiritually discern, but he can choose whether he listens to his moral conscience and whether he uses his senses to walk in righteousness or wickedness. On the other hand, animals have instincts and will not move from who they are or step outside of the programs that have been established within their makeup because to do so would mean the death of a species.

Creation declares the obvious that there is a Creator and that He has created all things to function within a divine order to ensure a perfect environment, but man has stepped outside of it and now all of creation mourns under the grave weight of sin and oppression. The question is, has it fared well for man to step outside of the order and purpose his Creator has ordained for him? For Adam it led to death and for the generations that followed, it has led to the breakup of families, the ruin of societies, and the destruction of nations.[16]

Imagine if you were in Elihu's shoes being clearly rebuked by your Creator. In a sense you would serve as an example of what not to do, and that is to never start from the foolish pinnacle of opinionated arrogance. It is clear that God put Elihu's knowledge in a humble perspective, silencing any further debate on his part. There are things a man may know and there are things that a man may learn, but there are also matters a man will know nothing about and when he inserts himself as an expert in such matters, he will discover soon enough that he knows absolutely nothing outside of providential wisdom. It is the wise man that understands this fact and has learned the disciplines of restraints: that opinions come from pride, platitudes reveal ignorance, and speculation

---

[15] The Evolution of a Creationist, pgs. 202-205
[16] Romans 1:20-25; 5:12-14; 8:20-23

serves as boomerangs that will come back to expose heart attitudes and personal judgments. These boomerangs will come back in judgment to the culprit after being flung at unsuspecting "offenders."

God was not through presenting His case. It was at this point His presentation was directed at another. He would not be humbling the arrogant, but rather challenging one to come higher. The righteous are counted righteous not because of what they have done but because of God's glorious, sovereign grace.

It is always interesting to see how different people respond to the Lord's reproof. The arrogant will be brought down, the sinner will become fearful, the wicked will be silenced, but the righteous—well, they are another story altogether.

Who Will Contend?
(Job 40-41)

Charles Spurgeon stated, "They who navigate little streams and shallow creeks, know but little of the God of tempests; but they who 'do business in great waters,' these see 'His wonders in the deep.' Among the huge Atlantic-waves of bereavement, poverty, temptation, and reproach, we learn the power of Jehovah, because we feel the littleness of man." Any revelation of God will cause man to see that at best he is a very small dot in the scheme of things.

The tone changes in Job 40 as the Lord takes a short pause and redirects His focus. If Job was relaying the Lord's words to Elihu, those present would have heard the Lord's rebuke. However, Job's response in Job 40:4-5 was quite telling as to who the Lord was talking to when He posed the next question. The Lord asked up front, "Who is he that contends with the Almighty by instructing Him?" He went on to challenge anyone who would dare reprove Him, to let him answer now. It was Job who answered the Lord, "Behold, I am vile; what shall I answer thee? I will lay mine hand upon my mouth. Once have I spoken; but I will not answer; yea, twice; but I will proceed no further."

It is interesting to see how people respond to God once they hear His voice. The sinner will be fearful, the wicked will be silenced, the evil will try to sneak away to avoid the light exposing them, and the righteous will humble themselves and take responsibility for what is being brought forth in the light of truth.

The question is, did Job contend with the Almighty? "Contend" points to the concept of wrestling while you are trying to nail down your opponent. We know that Job wrestled **before** the Lord as he debated with his companions as to the reason behind his plight, but did he step over the line and like Jacob when wrestling **with** God at Jabbok to receive a blessing? Jacob received his blessing, but his hip was knocked out of joint.[17]

Job appeared bold at times when his faith was taking flight, but was his boldness a bit too brash that it was close to stepping over the line of disrespect? Moses was pretty bold when he approached God in Numbers 14:11-25, but that was on behalf of Israel. Job had no intercessor and as believers we are told to boldly approach the throne of grace seeking mercy.[18]

However, Job was not seeking mercy because of some sin but desired insight as to what was behind his plight. His reason for it was honorable. He wanted to make sure he was not in some sin. Would God hold that as an offense against Job or would He use it as a means to go even deeper in the character and faith of Job? Author Bob Sorge said it best, "God wants to break us of our self-reliance and produce in us a deep humility and profound dependency upon Him. In a word, it's called brokenness."

---

[17] Genesis 32:24-32
[18] Hebrew 4:16

God's insertion in a matter would produce the same responses from any righteous person: humility and brokenness. Righteous people take to heart God's exhortations. The exhortation might not personally apply to them, but it is truth that God took time to personally address; therefore, it must be noted as a point of godly discipline to be applied at the appropriate time. Since the righteous people are actually prepared to respond to God in an honorable way, any encounter with God leaves them undone, unable to answer, and often broken. They may not sense conviction of personal sin, but they have a profound sense as to how far from the mark of a holy God they are and that they are scarcely saved. This profound sense is what will break them, sometimes in unexpected ways. In fact, each new revelation will cause some type of breaking in the righteous person, often causing great dread to the soul.[19]

Job had right standing before the Lord, but at times we believers can forget that there is a difference between right standing **before** the Lord and right standing **in** the Lord. When unfairly put on the defense we can get caught up with pointing out our actions, instead of standing on the abiding assurance that our life is not defined by actions, but by our relationship with God. It is our upright position in the Lord that serves as the source of all that is counted as being righteous.

All righteousness comes from the Lord. He alone counts a matter for righteousness, which allows obedient action to become acceptable to Him. If obedience is not a matter of faith, the action can't be counted as righteous. Job stood righteous because God counted his faith as being righteous; therefore, counted his obedient acts as being acceptable. However, without the garments of true righteousness covering a person, he or she will

---

[19] Genesis 28;12-17; Isaiah 6:1-6; 1 Peter 4:18

stand naked and without recourse before that which will become a consuming fire to anything that is profane.[20]

It is clear that in the Lord's first discourse, He was dealing with a prideful upstart. We know that if pride exists it will be brought low, but what does He do in relationship to the righteous who have been buried under a series of challenges? The Lord will challenge their perspective.

I have discovered this bit of truth in my own life. When I thought I could not go any further, the Lord showed me the way of Calvary and the grave that ended in His resurrection. When I wanted to sit in the middle of the road and give up, He told me to choose. My choice was between the plush valleys of Sodom and Gomorrah and the fiery oven of Shadrach, Meshach, and Abednego. When I was spiritually bankrupt, He reminded me that He gave up His glory to become poor so I could become rich in spiritual matters. When I felt my back was up against the wall, He showed me that His back was against the cross.

God was not rebuking Job as much as challenging him to look beyond the circumstances to something much greater. Perspective is everything when it comes to properly viewing that which can't be seen with the physical eye. Keep in mind, before God personally addressed Job, He had just made reference to the eagle, a bird that has incredible perspective because of the great heights it can reach. Man may not be able to see the eagle when it has reached its great height with the naked eye, but the eagle will see man. Even though perspective has been addressed in this book, it is vital that we identify it as the very point where God would challenge Job. He was about to call him higher.

In what way would God challenge Job's perspective? In His address to Elihu, He challenged him with aspects of His creation that he could not explain or predict. Such matters will knock

---

[20] Romans 4:12-14; 1 Corinthians 1:30; Hebrews 12:28,29

arrogant know-it-all's off of any lofty pinnacle, but how will He challenge Job's perspective? He will do it with those parts of creation that will reveal aspects of His majesty.

There are facets of creation that will bring awe and wonderment to one's soul. They can be admired but never explained. They can give one a sense of God's bigness and power while making one aware of the intricate details that God put in every one of His designs, once again pointing to God's incredible sovereignty at work. The key is if God works such details in every one of His designs, then can we rightfully conclude that He is that intricate when it comes to our lives?

There is nothing that can redirect our perspective from that of circumstances better than glimpses of God's majesty. Our circumstances may be burying us, but in light of God's majesty they can quickly dissipate the darkness. These circumstances seem like they are the biggest hindrances in our life, but there is always something that can prove to be bigger, and past bigger is the incredible majesty of God.

A good example of bigness is Mount Everest. It is the highest point on the planet. Its peak pierces the roaring winds of the jet stream five miles above the earth, while casting a shadow that stretches for 250 miles. One writer, after seeing it from an airplane window, described how its magnificence, its absolute immensity made her hair stand on end for a week. It is the shadow or revelation of that which is incredible that makes man aware of his smallness, and at times experience great dread in facing the One the heavens can't even contain.

In God's creation it does not take something like a great mountain to mark great heights. The black and yellow garden spider has a unique way of traveling. It is known as "ballooning." This spider throws out streams of silk that form a sort of "flying carpet." It rises on warm currents of ascending air causing these spiders to be born aloft and scatter far and wide. Sometimes these "flying carpets" go as high as 14,000 to 15,000 feet and travel hundreds or even thousands of miles.[21] In fact, it is believed these "flying carpets" might be behind an international incident that was witnessed at a football game held in Tuscany, Italy October 27, 1954. It is suspected that many of these spider carpets merged together, appearing much like a UFO, and when this image disbursed, it left behind a sticky substance that could not be identified.

Before the Lord used His creation, (mainly two creatures) to challenge their perspective, He was about to reinsert Himself into the exhortation. Remember Job Chapter 40 started with a question to Job and Job responded, but now the Lord is once again going to speak out of the whirlwind.[22] This little detail may not seem to be important but it is very significant. Just as in the case of the first whirlwind, God may be addressing one man, but His exhortation is for all five men to hear.

There is power and intensity in whirlwinds and the reality of it is they declare one thing, and that is no mere man or even a group of men will be able to stand up against it. The whirlwind will have its way. In fact, the term "reaping the whirlwind" can be found in Hosea 8:7. A whirlwind will knock down that which is not on a sure foundation and it will cause all structures erected by man to be damaged, unhinged, torn asunder, and destroyed. Keep in mind, those who opposed Job based their conclusions on their dogma that, in many cases, had been passed down through the teachings of their fathers and accepted traditions, but when God steps on the scene to set the record straight it is often like a whirlwind that tears apart boxes of theology, strips assumed and presumed doctrine of any authority, upends any wrong conclusions, and

---

[21] The Evolution of a Creationist, pgs. 87-90
[22] Job 40:6

destroys any strongholds of ideas that ultimately exalt themselves against the real knowledge of who He is.[23]

The Lord once again commanded that one should gird up his loins like a man.[24] Was He talking to Job or was He talking to whoever would dare stand up and give an account of himself? Job already confessed that he would cease from speaking any further. To me, what follows implies He was talking to those present, but which one would own it, and who would allow it to make a lasting impact on his attitude?

The first thing He asks is if a person can disannul His judgments and in ignorance condemn Him so they can appear righteous.[25] Which men or what man were disannulling God's judgments? People disannul God's judgments when they interpret them to the point that they make His ultimate judgment unrecognizable or invalid, giving the impression they are more just than the Lord, while misrepresenting Him. Four of these men clearly fell into this category.

Job did not understand what was going on but he knew he was not under some judgment. His unwillingness to admit wrong, was not a judgment leveled at God, neither did his claims of being justified exalt him above the Lord.

The Lord continued to present His case. Does man have an arm like Him that can reach into hell itself or into the eternal heights to bring about a matter? Does man have a voice that can be heard throughout all that exists in heaven and on earth? Can man array himself with such majesty and glory as He, or cast aside His anger or rage? Can they abase the proud and bring them low, as well as put the wicked in their appropriate place?[26] It was clear that the companions of Job were trying to make their voice heard,

---

[23] 2 Corinthians 10:3-5
[24] Job 40:7
[25] Job 40:8
[26] Job 40:9-12

array themselves with wisdom and righteousness, represent God's anger, and bring Job low in order to put him in his appropriate place, while exalting their conclusions.

The statement that follows in Job 10:14 is a culmination of the impact of man in all spiritual matters, "Then will I also confess unto thee that thine own right hand can save thee." In other words, if a man could do such feats, he would be able to save himself, but there is only One who can save and that is the God of the universe.

The Lord will only speak of two creatures in the next two chapters to prove His point. One is the behemoth. This creature eats grass, but he has great strength in his loins, moves his tail like a cedar and his sinews are wrapped and twisted together like rope. His bones are like tubes of bronze, his ribs like bars of iron and he is chief as to the ways of God. He lies under the tree for shade, allowing the reeds and ferns to hide him and the willow of the brook compasses him. This creature is able to drink up the river and no one can take him when he is watching, and who can reach him to even pierce him through the nose.[27]

There is much speculation about this plant-eating creature who needed a wet environment to live. Some speculate it is an elephant or hippopotamus, but both fail to meet the full description of the animal. However, there is one creature that possesses every one of these characteristics: a dinosaur.

There is proof that man and dinosaurs walked together before the flood, and since creatures don't live for hundreds of years as before the flood, and the present-day oxygen levels could not maintain such a large creature, it is believed that some of these creatures adapted and could still be among us, but in smaller forms.[28]

---

[27] Job 40:15-24
[28] See the book, "Footprints and the Stones of Time."

When we talk about something big, we automatically associate great strength to it. It is true strength usually follows that which is big, but there is something else in creation that is five times stronger than steel and twice as strong as Kevlar, the material used to make bulletproof vest of the same weight. In fact, one strand the size of a pencil of this material could stop a 747 in flight, and what is this incredible substance? I have already mentioned the creature that produces this silk-like substance which it uses to make unique and strong webs: A spider.

The next creature the Lord mentions in Job 41 is the leviathan. This is also another controversial creature. Keep in mind, God would not have mentioned these two creatures if the men present did not know about them. Many believe this creature is the crocodile, and from some of its characteristics it could very well fit the description, but once again there are characteristics that can't be accredited to the present-day crocodile.

The leviathan is a sea creature; however, no man can catch him, tame him, or play with him. No device of man can lay claim to him and if a man ever did manage to somehow take hold of him, he would never do it again. This creature lays low, hidden from the naked eye of man and if an individual manages to come upon him, he dares not stir him up.[29]

It is at this point the Lord asks in the last part of Job 41:10, "Who then is able to stand before me?" Concerning the first creature, the Lord makes it clear that unless He brings the Behemoth to man, man is not able to take it down, and if this creature is watching, man is never able to sneak up on it.[30] God's sovereignty determines when and how man will be involved in a matter. If God does not permit it, it will never happen and if man is able to accomplish a matter it is because He allows it.

---

[29] Job 41:1-10
[30] Job 40:19, 24; 41:10

The second aspect about God's sovereignty has to do with His judgments. Like the leviathan, no one can tame, direct, and control His judgments. Like the behemoth man may be able to observe His **ways** but he will never be able to corner, surprise, or undermine God's ways for they are higher than man's ways.[31] And, when it comes to the reason behind God's **judgments**, like the leviathan they are hidden, and for those who try to take hold of them for their own benefit, will discover quickly that it will not fare well for them. God alone disburses His judgments, and in the end, no one will be able to stand before Him. The Lord actually confirms this in Job 41:11, "Who hath prevented me, that I should repay him? whatsoever is under the whole heaven is mine." In essence the Lord was asking who has prevented Him in His work and who can demand repayment for His ways of dealing with man since all of creation belongs to Him?

If man could get away with it, he would take God to court over those things of creation that caused him loss, harm, and despair, but the truth is man has no case against God because he came into this world as a stranger, benefited from the blessings of God along the way, and ultimately will not be able to take anything with him when he leaves this world behind.

The Lord makes it clear that He will not conceal the leviathan parts, his power or the greatness of his frame.[32] He wants people to understand the greatness of this creature for they will be without excuse if they ever find themselves tangling with it. Likewise, God has not hid His part in salvation, kept His power secret, or shrouded His greatness. It can be seen in all of creation.

He talked about the creature's skin, jaws and the horribleness of its sharp teeth. He speaks about how the leviathan' scales serve as its protection and prove to be the source of pride for they

---

[31] Isaiah 55:8-9
[32] Job 41:12

seal him in. His scales are joined together like armor that can't be penetrated, preventing him from being subdued. Apparently, his nostrils shoot out fire and smoke, his eyes are reddish and fire leaps out of his mouth.[33]

As the Lord continued to describe this creature, the leviathan appears to become more mythical, but the truth is there are legends in different cultures about fire-breathing dragons. There are also modern-day sightings of great creatures that swim in our waters. There are those who say that there is no creature living today that could emit such fire and smoke, but there is such a creature.

The Bombardier Beetle ejects an acrid fluid which is discharged with a distinct popping sound and a small cloud of vapor that looks like the smoke from a miniature cannon. This substance is cross between tear gas and a tommy gun and when the toxic substance explodes from its body, it does so at a boiling point of 212 F.[34]

The Lord points out the leviathan neck which displays great strength as terror dances before him. The folds of his flesh cleave together and can't be moved. His heart is strong and solid and when he rises up the mighty become afraid and when he begins to thrash about, man finds himself beside himself, without any recourse.[35]

This will prove to be true when the Lord rises up to judge. His strength will be on display and the mighty will become afraid and the rebellious will not know where to turn. Some will even ask the rocks to fall on them.[36]

No sword, spear, dart, and spear can touch him, while iron is like straw that falls to the wayside and brass like rotten wood that

---

[33] Job 41:13-21
[34] The Evolution of a Creationist, pgs. 39-42
[35] Job 41:22-25
[36] Revelation 6:12-17

crumbles when it hits the target. Arrows do not faze him, slingstones along with darts are turned into stubble, and he laughs at the shaking of the spear.[37]

His underparts are like sharp pieces of broken pottery that make a path wherever he goes. He causes the deep to boil like a pot and the sea like a pot of ointment. He leaves a distinct path behind him.[38]

It becomes clear that there is none like this creature on earth, but there is none like the Lord God. This creature beholds all high things marked by pride for he is a king over all of the children of pride.[39]

It is believed that the leviathan is a type of Satan. There is none like Satan and he is king over all children of pride. It is the children of pride that exalt themselves, stand tall in their own eyes, tout greatness, believe themselves to be infallible, and refuse to be wrong.

However, when it comes to man, Satan is untouchable and would leave man helpless, defenseless, and hopeless if God did not put boundaries on him. Hell is the devil's domain, green sulfur is his ointment, and utter destruction is the path he leaves behind.

God did not explain that Satan was behind Job's plight, but by ending with this creature, perhaps He was casting a shadow that allowed the discerning Job to see who he was up against. After all, Satan's ways are hidden from man, and man has no idea he is there until this great adversary leaves some type of calling card. When Satan breathes out his lies, he leaves man helpless, when he sends forth the fire of his slanderous accusations, he leaves man defenseless, and when he isolates man in utter despair, he leaves him hopeless.

---

[37] Job 41:26-29
[38] Job 41:30-32
[39] Job 41:33,34

Satan reigns with terror, but as soon as God steps on the scene, he must once again hide himself in the depths of darkness, that is until the next test of man's faith is highlighted as a target. Such targets are what make man's soul a battleground between the Redeemer of his soul and the fierce enemy of his soul.

The Testimony
(Job 42)

After the Lord's exhortation, who would speak? Job would respond. We need to keep in mind that Job is the story of a man, who because of his faith towards God, became a target of Satan. The great struggle in this world is not over kingdoms, but souls. Job's soul became a battle ground between two diverse kingdoms as circumstances buried him and friends persecuted him, but his faith towards the Lord would not let him give up nor would his integrity allow him to surrender to a false narrative. As we are about to see, his faith led him through the darkness engulfing his soul to discover the ultimate treasure.

It is clear that God's rebuke was towards Job's companions, but He was clearly challenging Job's perspective. As stated before, the righteous will own a truth, take it to heart, and let it go deep into their soul like a sharp knife, producing a profound sense of brokenness as to just how little they are and how far away they are from the mark of God's holiness.

Every revelation of the Lord's greatness will leave a righteous person completely undone, and after emerging from the fiery trials of their faith, they are ready to fling the remaining smoking rags aside to embrace the promises of God. Out of each trial comes a greater awareness of God and when the smoke and sweet fragrance lifts from the altar of the heart, the saint finds something so precious and beautiful remaining, that of a greater testimony of their Maker.

Consider what the righteous Job confessed in Job 42:2. He first admitted what he already knew, that the Lord can do all things and that no thought can be hidden from Him. Job went on to acknowledge that God does not hide any counsel without first giving understanding and that he, Job, spoke without understanding what was really going on. He now recognized that what was taking place behind the scene was so wonderful that there was no way he could have known.[40]

Remember, for the righteous it is about perspective and at this point, we can clearly see that Job's perspective had been transformed. Yes, he lost it all, but it was in light of God doing something more wonderful than he could have imagined. Even though Job desired an explanation from God, it was the Lord who demanded an explanation from man because the Potter does not have to answer the vessel, but at times the vessel must give an account of itself to the Potter when it has lost its way or is missing the mark.

It is important that we realize Job was giving a record or testimony of God. He was able to now declare what was hidden from him in the fiery ovens as being so. He was no longer focusing on what happened to him but the grace and wondrous working of God behind the scenes, and it is at this point that Job is able to declare the result of his incredible test of faith, "I have heard of thee by the hearing of the ear: but now mine eye seeth thee."

Job wanted to hear an explanation, but at the end of his faith he did not receive an explanation; rather, he received an incredible revelation of God. In the past he had heard of his Creator's greatness but now he was allowed to see God's greatness in action through His workings in and through creation.

Job saw God's incredible wisdom in His designs on the canvas of creation. His omnipotence in bringing forth all creation in a

---

[40] Job 42:3

perfect order was on display, His omniscience in knowing the smallest details to the greatest happenings were pointed out, and the fact He is omnipresence, ever present in all matters became obvious. Job was allowed to see God's perfect ways and His righteous judgments in two unlikely creatures. He caught glimpses of His sovereignty in the workings of the unusual, His humor with the curious, His imagination in the unexplainable, and His majesty in the incredible.

In light of such an awe-inspiring revelation, Job could only do one thing, abhor himself and repent in dust and ashes. Job came face to face with his humanness and it does not matter how right you do things, it is that element of being human that is going to remind you that there are always aspects of your character that will ultimately miss the mark of your high calling, and that even in an upright status, the fact still remains, the righteous are scarcely saved. At such times repentance is not about turning from sin, but recognizing just how small you are in the scheme of things and that there is no good thing in you. The conclusion at such times is the same: The safest place to be is ever looking up from a state of humility, ready to face God while recognizing that it is indeed His grace that keeps and preserves you.

After God had finished with His prophet, Job, He still had some unfinished business. In His first discord He took care of the upstart, Elihu. Not only was this novice put in his proper place to once again sit at the end of the table of insignificance, but he was silenced and perhaps prepared to learn about the deep things of God. However, the three companions of Job who knew the truth and set the stage for terrible injustices to be leveled at Job had not been specifically addressed. Such individuals can always remain on the outside fringes debating as to whether they brought truth and edification to a matter. They often perceive that they have missed the bullet because God's attention is not directed at them.

Jeannie Schantz made this statement, "Those who have only read but have not lived the book of Job cannot imagine the stress on a struggling human heart which, held powerless by His power, is still required to trust the love it cannot see and to pray for the friends who have not been friends at all." Job was clearly placed in this position.

God specifically directed His attention at Job's friends and spoke to Eliphaz. He told him that His wrath was kindled against him and his other two companions for they had not spoken of Him the things that were right like His servant Job. His command was for them to take seven bullocks and seven rams and go to Job and offer them up for a burnt offering and Job would pray for them, and then for Job's sake He would receive their offering.[41]

I want you to think about what is being said here. These men needed a daysman to stand in the gap for them before God could accept any offering from them, and who would be that daysman? It was Job, the very man who desired them to be his intercessors. It would be upon Job's prayer that the Lord would honor their sacrifices so they would not have to taste His wrath. Can you imagine the bitter taste these men had to swallow? But if I was in their shoes, I would much more fear God's wrath than choking down the bitterness of my pride. The three companions did as the Lord commanded and Job stood in the gap and God accepted his intercession on behalf of his three friends.

We are told that after praying for his friends, the Lord turned Job's captivity into a double portion of blessings. If the blessings were as fair as his three daughters, they had to be incredible. We know that he lived 140 years after his great ordeal and that he died, being old and full of days.[42]

---

[41] Job 42:7-9
[42] Job 42:10,15-17

Through Job's indelible testimony of faith, he lives on. His challenging book is like a lake where you can clearly see where it starts and ends, along with its transparent bottom, but you can't judge the depth of it. And, when you jump in to see if you can touch its bottom, you find that it is so much further than you imagined. You find yourself having to come up for air, gasping as you strive to stay afloat. You must not quit attempting to reach the depths because you have caught glimpses of great treasures simply resting on the bottom, and it is not enough for you to know they are there or to simply admire them, you must take possession of them. However, each time you dive into the water to reach the treasures, you realize you will never be able to fully possess them because they prove to be just beyond your reach.

Job has taught me that is the way of God's sovereignty. Its workings are marked by some event and ultimately its ends will be obvious, but its depths are too great and its heights are too far to reach. Even though His sovereignty is made transparent by His truth and contains riches beyond description, these riches can never be fully possessed. The reason is because the depths and heights of His sovereignty always come back to that which is beyond measurement and reaches into that which is eternal in order to unveil that which is glorious and beyond description and explanation.

14

A Final Thought

Christian suffering is the
crucible into which God places us,
and in which He keeps us until
He can see a reflection
of the face of Jesus Christ in
our lives.
(Kenneth Wuest)

As we come to the close of this journey with Job through his book, I want to thank each reader for taking it with me. I have touched the surface and perhaps gone deeper into that bottomless lake I mentioned in the last chapter, and yet it still proves overwhelming to my finite mind. Every time I take this journey, I discover more treasures. Each new discovery reminds me that I must continue to take this journey through Job to discover more treasures, but I also take it to prepare myself to advance into the four poetic books that follow.

There are two books that many in American Christendom avoid: the book of Job and The Song of Solomon. There are those who have truly valued these books and taught on them. For example, in the oriental culture, the Song of Solomon is widely prized due to eastern customs that are evident in the book. And, when it comes to those who greatly suffer, the book of Job becomes a wonderful book of consolation and hope.

As mentioned in my introduction, both of these books are part of the five poetic books that are positioned in the middle of the 66 books of the Canon. To be poetic, there must be a mixture of philosophy that explores life, emotional crescendos that mark changes in mood and tempo based on experiences in life, wisdom that brings enlightenment, reality that causes one to realistically face a matter, and if the search is centered around and on God, one discovers the highest of all virtues—that of godly love.

Job clearly possessed this mixture. It is the first book to mark this unique division in the Bible while the Song of Solomon is the last of the five poetic books. Through each book the strands of God's grace weave together an incredible picture, beginning with Job's great faith and ending with a simple handmaiden experiencing lasting love. In between these two books are the Psalms which can play every emotional heartstring while causing one to reach heights of ecstasy, only to fall into the depths of utter despair to once again be raised up with an inspirational crescendo that becomes the means to land on incredible hope and promises.

The book of Proverbs follows with wisdom that can cause one to become reasonable, balanced, and realistic about life. The contrasts in Proverbs are clearly inspired by simplicity, instructive in light of the practical, and profound in relationship as to the depths and loftiness the reader can obtain by always reaching for heights of wisdom that will bring one to places of excellence.

Ecclesiastes leads one to land on the reality of this life. All that is attached to this world, which includes preferences, lifestyles, and pursuits are nothing more than vanity. This vanity causes people to know leanness of spirit, disillusionment, hopelessness in life, and emptiness in pursuits. The only conclusion that the teacher could reach at the end of the book was simple, "Let us hear the conclusion of the whole matter: Fear God, and keep his commandments: for this is the whole *duty* of man. For God shall bring every work into judgment, with every secret thing, whether it be good, and whether it be evil."[1]

In the Song of Solomon, the stages of love are revealed in order to lead a person into the revelation of the enduring love of that which is mature and eternal. It speaks of intimate relationship that in reality God so desires to have with His people.

When I read the Bible, my main goal is to see Jesus in the shadows cast in each of the Old Testament books. In order to unveil Him in His ways, I seek to follow the patterns that lead me to a greater revelation of God.[2]

Job's book prepares for the emotional roller coaster of Psalms that ends in lows but experiences the highs, while, as with Proverbs, seeks for wisdom in the midst of the ridiculous, and similarly to Ecclesiastes, recognizes the vanity of the age. Ultimately, like the Song of Solomon it lands on the reality that when it comes to God it is all about right relationship.

Does Job cast any real shadow that can somehow open a door to a pattern that can be followed? Job does cast a shadow. There was a man in the New Testament who was perfect, upright, feared God, and hated evil so much He became sin for each one of us. He walked among men working righteousness, but was betrayed by a friend, falsely accused by the religious, mocked by the scorners, and disdained by the skeptical. He became a man of sorrow and faced a great night of testing without any intercessor and when it was all over, He became an intercessor for all of us. His name is Jesus Christ.[3]

Is there a pattern that emerges into an incredible story? For each person who seeks the pattern, the story may vary, but this is the pattern I discovered for my edification. For the book of Job, it

[1] Ecclesiastes 12:13,14
[2] Hebrews 8:5
[3] Isaiah 53:4,5; 2 Corinthians 5:21; Hebrews 4:15; 7:25,26; 1 Peter 1:18,19; 2:21-22; 1 John 3:5

begins with one man and exposes and explores the different philosophies of life, which are greatly influenced by family, religious influences, and friends. However, in the classroom of the world, life, the teacher teaches the righteous person that man holds few answers, understands little, knows nothing of real significance, and when put against the wall of a matter is incapable of answering the most basic questions of life. Life reveals that outside of the design, workings, and plan of the Creator, man is void of answers, resolutions, or solutions. Man will begin with what he thinks he knows, only to realize he knows nothing of the unseen until it is revealed to him. If man fails to end with the reality of God, he will discover himself to be a fool without an intercessor.

Once man begins with the reality of God, he can move to the Psalms where the prophetic forthtelling in relationship to the challenges of man and foretelling in light of the promises of God is woven into emotional experiences. Man is meant to experience life, but real life can only be experienced when man tastes the goodness of the Lord, delights in His law, knows His protection, rests in His safety, is touched by His presence, enfolded by joy unspeakable, and embraces His salvation. As man experiences the good, the bad, the unpredictable, the sorrowful, and joyful aspects of life, he must remember to look up during great challenges, while waiting for the storms to pass, the winds to cease, the clouds to part, and the light to shine through to see that there is a silver lining in the midst of life's challenges called redemption. This incredible act connects his past experience with his present happenings to shape his future according to the hope and promises of resurrection and the next age to come. King David summarized it best in Psalm 17:15, "As for me, I will behold thy face in righteousness: I shall be satisfied, when I awake, with thy likeness."

Proverbs is about walking out the godly life according to heavenly wisdom, while Ecclesiastes warns the saint to avoid falling into the trap of vanity and the Song of Solomon unveils the great revelation for all who dare walk the narrow path of life: the incredible love of God.

The Bible is about lining us up to God's righteous ways. Job is about faith that ensures righteousness, Psalms point to the inspiration and expectation that allows one to experience the ways of righteousness, Proverbs reveal the discretion that helps one to discern the fruits of righteousness, Ecclesiastes shows the needs and benefits of righteousness in light of vanity, and the Song of Solomon speaks of godly love that disciplines the ways of righteousness.

The journey the poetic books take the reader on began with one man and that is true about each of us. Our spiritual journey begins with us as an individual soul, and how far we get in this journey and whether we finish it, will come down to the level of our faith towards the true God of the universe and whether we receive the truth about one man, the Lord Jesus Christ.

Jesus went to the cross where He paid for our sins in order to reconcile us back to God. We must approach His redemption by simple faith that believes the Word is true to be saved. We must learn that life outside of God and His love is vanity and that it is in grave darkness we will receive a greater revelation of Him.

Faith is the only response that pleases God, allowing Him to count it as righteous along with subsequent actions. This is why faith must go through a process to bring forth its value and the Bible reveals that process, especially in the life of Job and the prophets. We are to exhort souls to continue in the faith since we must through much tribulation enter into the kingdom of God. We are told by Paul if we are to be heirs with the Lord, we must suffer with Him and that all who live godly in Christ Jesus shall be persecuted. The apostle Peter explained why faith is associated with tribulation, adversity, and suffering in 1 Peter 5:10, "But the God of all grace who hath called us unto his eternal glory by Christ Jesus, after that ye have suffered a while, make you perfect, stablish, strengthen, settle you?" [4]

Faith therefore must be tested in fiery ovens, refined in adversity, and enlarged by revelation to ensure one runs the race, endures the terrain, finishes the course, and becomes part of the great cloud of witness.[5] This means that the walk of faith will not only lead you up to the fiery ovens, but it will lead you out of them into a realm of darkness while disciplining your feet to walk a slippery course you can't even see. It will take you into deep formidable places that can bring terror to the senses, despair to the emotions, and insanity to the mind. It will bring into question everything you thought you knew, believed, and stood on.

It ultimately costs to become heirs of faith that obtain the promises, but as Job would clearly testify, it will prove to be worth it in the end. It is true that this great man of faith grappled with his confusing philosophy, wrestled with his crumbling theology, and encountered despair before his useless ideology, but his faith allowed him to land in the only place that made sense, and that was on what he knew to be true about his Creator.

My faith walk constantly teaches me it is about the inheritance and the spiritual legacy that is tied into a great cloud of witnesses. Faith identifies believers to the inheritance and causes them to walk according to their spiritual legacy. The walk of faith disciplines each of our steps, the ways of faith prepares us to receive, the expectation of faith transforms our attitude, and the hope of faith conforms us to the life that is being developed in us. Job's faith had led him to the place where he could see what his real lasting portion of his inheritance was and as a result his

---

[4] Acts 14:22; Romans 4:3; 8:17; 2 Timothy 2:12; Hebrews 11:6; James 5:10,11
[5] 2 Timothy 4:7; Hebrews 12:1; 1 Peter 1:5-9

spiritual legacy became part of the great cloud of witnesses. And, what is that witness, "I have heard of you, but now I have seen you."

As a believer in Jesus Christ, I am steadfastly walking towards one destination where I will obtain the end of my faith, that of my salvation. And with great joy, adoration, and worship, I will be assured of seeing and possessing the real portion of my spiritual inheritance which is summarized in1 John 3:2, "…when he shall appear, we shall be like him; for we shall see him as he is."

Bibliography

Strong's Exhaustive Concordance of the Bible © 1890 by James Strong, as well as 1980, 1986 assigned to World Bible Publishers, Inc.

Smith's Bible Dictionary, William Smith, L.L.D., © 1986 by Thomas Nelson, Inc

Baffled to Fight Better, Oswald Chambers, © 1931 and 1990 by Oswald Chambers Publications Associations Limited

The Privileged Planet, © 2004 by Guilermo Gonzalez and Jay W. Richards, Regnery Publishing

The Remarkable Record of Job, © 1988, 2000 by Henry M. Morris, Master Books, Inc.

God the Master Mathematician, © 2002 by Dr. N. W. Hutchings, Bible Belt Publishing

Halley's Bible Handbook, Henry H. Halley, 23rd edition © 1962, 24th edition © 1965, Zondervan Publishing House

Our Night Sky, Edward M. Murphy, Ph.D., © 2010 by The Teaching Company, Published by The Great Courses

The Great Pyramid Prophecy in Stone, © 1996, 2010 by Noah Hutchings, Defender Publishing

Footprints and the Stones of Time, © 1992 by Dr. Carl Baugh

Knothole Glimpses of Glory, F. Ellsworth Powell, © 1963 by Osterhus Publishing House

God Divided the Nations, © 1998 by Noah W. Hutchings, Hearthstone Publishing

The Puzzle of Ancient Man, Third Edition © 2006 by Donald E. Chittick, Published by Creation Compass

Tower of Babel, (The Cultural History of Our Ancestors) © 2012 by Bodie Hodge, Master Books

The Evolution of a Creationist, © 1994, 2002, 2004 by Dr. Jobe Martin.

Original Meaning of Scriptural Names, © 1949 by Lucy Bates

World History Chart in Accordance with Bible Chronology, © 2012

The Fire of Delayed Answers © 1996 by Bob Sorge, Oasis House

Other books by Rayola Kelley:

Hidden Manna
Battle for the Soul
Stories of the Heart
Transforming Love & Beyond
Post to Post: (1) Establishing the Way
Post to Post: (2) Walking in the Way

Volume One: Establishing Our Life in Christ
My Words are Spirit and Life
The Anatomy of Sin
The Principles of the Abundant Life
The Place of Covenant
Unmasking the Cult Mentality

Volume Two: Putting on the Life of Christ
He Actually Thought It Not Robbery
Revelation of the Cross
In Search of Real Faith
Think on These Things
Follow the Pattern

Volume Three: Developing a Godly Environment
Godly Discipline
Prayer and Worship
Don't Touch That Dial
Face of Thankfulness
ABC's of Christianity

Volume Four: Issues of the Heart
Hidden Manna (Revised)
Bring Down the Sacred Cows
The Manual for the Single Christian Life
Parents are People Too

Volume Five: Challenging the Christian Life
The Issues of Life
Presentation of the Gospel
For the Purpose of Edification
Whatever Happened to the Church?
Women's Place in the Kingdom of God

Volume Six: Developing Our Christian Life
The Many Faces of Christianity
Possessing Our Souls
Experiencing the Christian Life
The Power of Our Testimonies
The Victorious Journey

Volume Seven: Discovering True Ministry
From Prisons and Dots to Christianity
So You Want to be in Ministry

Devotions:
Devotions of the Heart: Book One and Two
Daily Food for the Soul: OT and NT

Gentle Shepherd Ministries Devotion Series:
Being a Child of God
Disciplining the Strength of our Youth
Coming to Full Age

Nugget Books:
Nuggets From Heaven
More Nuggets From Heaven
Heavenly Gems
More Heavenly Gems
Heavenly Treasures

Gentle Shepherd Ministries Series:
The Christian Life Series:
What Matter Is This?
The Challenge of It
The Reality of It

The Leadership Series:
Overcoming
A Matter of Authority and Power
The Dynamics of True Leadership

www.ingramcontent.com/pod-product-compliance
Lightning Source LLC
LaVergne TN
LVHW051502080426
835509LV00017B/1877